Mediterranean Style

MEDITERRANEAN STYLE

Relaxed living inspired by strong colour and natural materials

CATHERINE HAIG

First published in 1997 by
Conran Octopus Limited
a part of Octopus Publishing Group
2–4 Heron Quays, London E14 4JP

Reprinted 1998, 1999

Editorial Director: Suzannah Gough
Senior Editor: Catriona Woodburn
Editorial Assistant: Paula Hardy
Art Editors: Alison Fenton and Tony Seddon
Stylist: Emily Jewsbury
Special photography: Hannah Lewis
Picture Researcher: Rachel Davies
Production Controller: Julian Deeming

British Library Cataloguing-in-Publication Data:
A catalogue record for this book is available from the British Library.

ISBN 1 85029 916 1
Printed in China

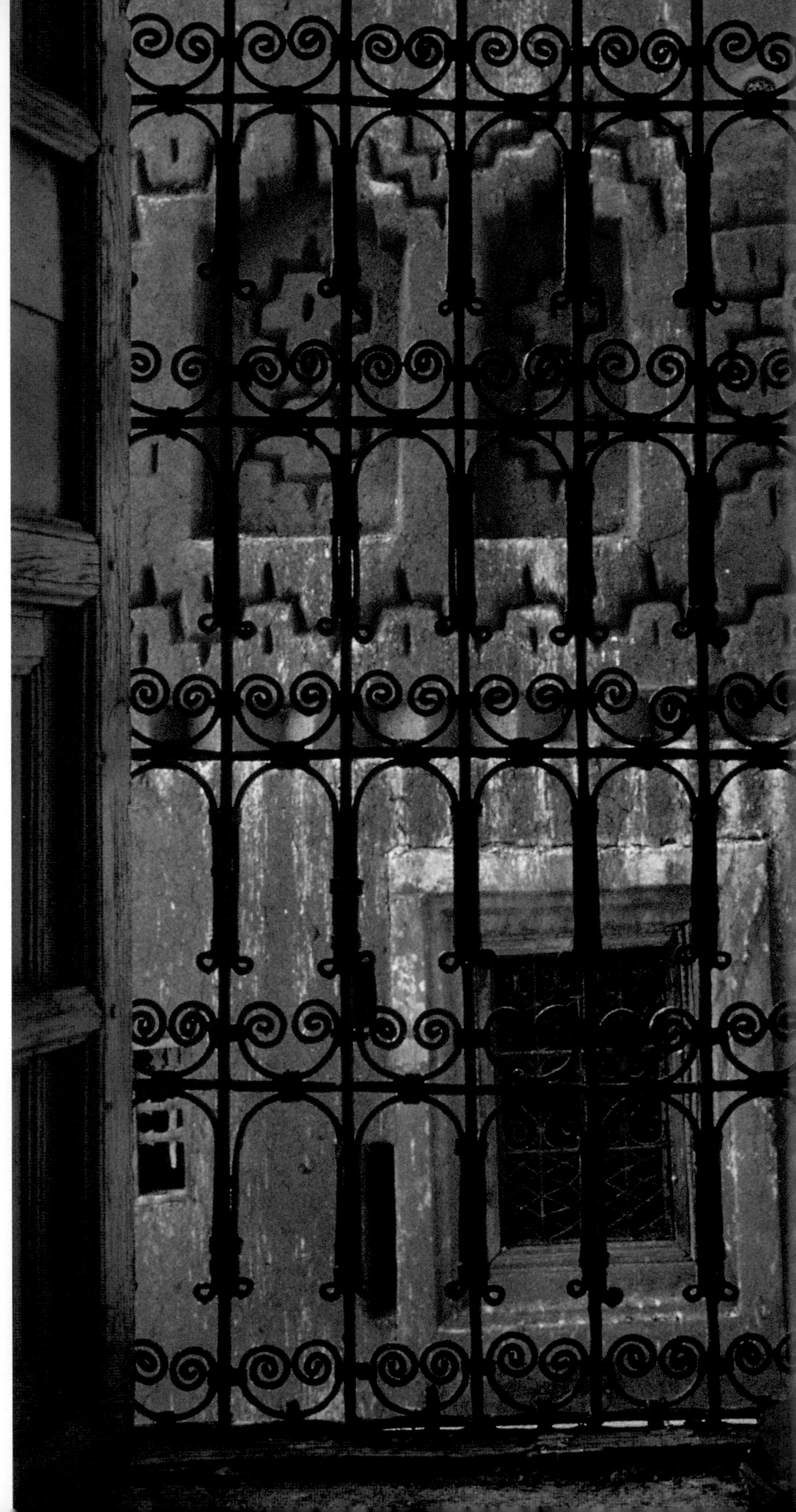

Contents

The Mediterranean Look

ORIGINS AND INFLUENCES

The Mediterranean has long been one of the great cultural and trading centres of the world, a historic meeting point for ideas and inspiration, for centuries the heart of Western civilization. Its name derives from the Latin for 'middle of the earth', and for the many peoples who have lived around its shores that is exactly what it once was.

In the words of Lawrence Durrell (1912–1990), 'The Mediterranean is an absurdly small sea; the length and greatness of its history make us dream it larger than it is'. This is borne out by even the most cursory glance into its past. It was the cradle of Christianity, which was founded on its eastern shores, and the foundation for some of the great empires of ancient times – the Persian, the Greek and the Roman. The legendary trading power of the Phoenicians and Carthaginians depended upon it and later, in the eighth century AD, the might of Islam swept right across it in the Moorish conquest of Spain. Control of these waters has played a vital part in virtually every European conflict since. Today, as a result of this political and religious diversity, the peoples of the Mediterranean profess a variety of faiths and speak approximately fifty different languages.

Over two thousand miles from end to end, the Mediterranean Sea is bordered by seventeen different countries. It is virtually landlocked, only linked with the Atlantic Ocean at its western end by the Strait of Gibraltar which is flanked by the two pillars of Hercules's mythological tenth labour, now known as Gibraltar to the north and Ceuta, in Morocco, to the south. At the eastern end, the Mediterranean issues through the even narrower Bosphorus into the (also landlocked) Black Sea and, since 1875, through the Suez Canal.

Over the centuries the natural and man-made wonders of the Mediterranean have inspired countless poets, writers and artists, and since the time of Dr Johnson (1709–1784), who wrote 'The grand object of travelling is to see the shores of the Mediterranean', they have proved a magnetic attraction for travellers from all over the world. In the eighteenth century, in the days of the Grand Tour, sons of the English well-to-do were dispatched to see the world, and the art and architecture of the Mediterranean exerted a powerful influence.

Early in the twentieth century the cosmopolitan rich and famous established resorts on the shores of the Mediterranean as a balmy escape from the rigours of the northern winter, and nowadays, with the advent of cheaper and easier international travel, millions of people flock to the region in search of the sun. Although they may see little more than a coastal resort and a stretch of sand littered with basking bodies, these contemporary travellers will undoubtedly be influenced – whether consciously or unconsciously – by the essence of the Mediterranean: the look, the colours, noises, smells and tastes.

Images of the beaches of Spain, the French and Italian rivieras, and the whitewashed villages nestling on the shores of Greek islands are only one facet of the Mediterranean. It also includes the drama of the Pyrenees, the swampy marshlands of the Camargue, the Atlas mountains of Morocco, the dusty aridity of Algeria, Libya and Egypt, the lushness of the Lebanon, and the marvellous contrasts on islands such as Cyprus where it is possible to ski the snowy slopes of the Troodos mountains in the morning and swim in the sea in the afternoon.

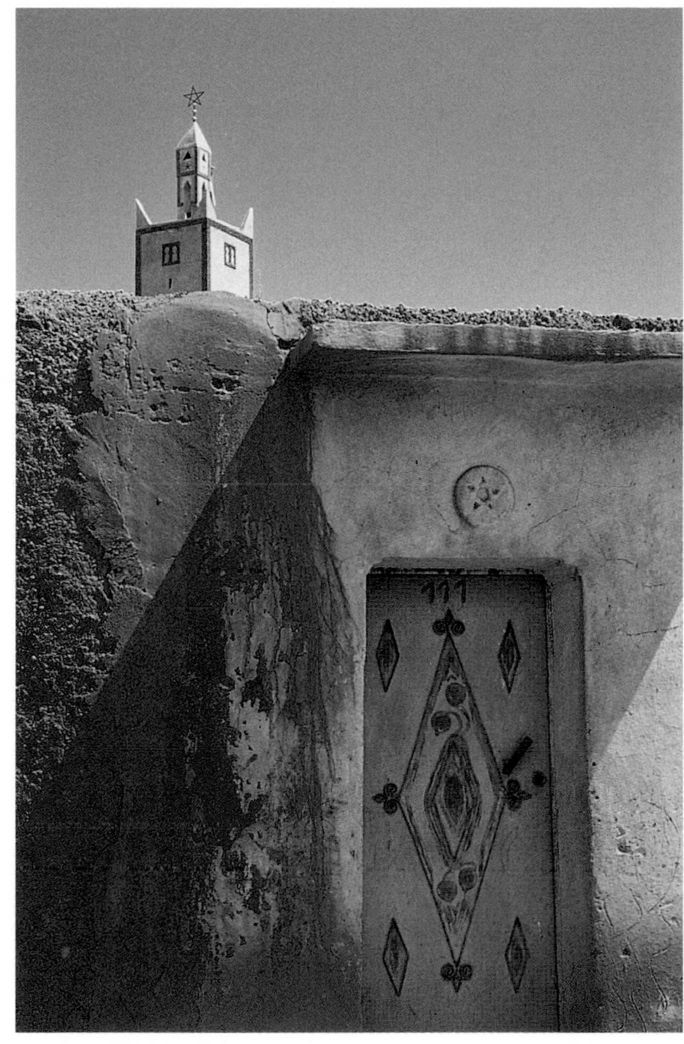

Above *A flamboyantly decorated door is set deep into a rustic wall, the earthy tones of paint and plaster standing boldly against a bright blue sky.*

Facing *A verdant Italian landscape with silvery-grey olive groves, emerald-green grass, and trees and shrubs in full flower on the hillside, is punctuated by the occasional, black-green cypress.*

Above *A characteristic view of a Mediterranean village: a patchwork of pantiled roofs and glimpses of terraces and balconies, tumbling down a Sicilian hillside.*

Facing *In an ancient village in the Chianti region of Italy, a mass of pale purple wisteria blossom curtains a rough stone wall below an arched loggia.*

It is not only the landscape – whether man-made or natural – that captures the soul; the flavours of the Mediterranean have also colonized cultures far beyond its geographical boundaries. In part this is due to improved communications, which today allow fresh fruit and vegetables to be exported worldwide, and in part to the pioneering cookery writings of the likes of Elizabeth David, whose first book, *Mediterranean Cookery* (1950), encouraged the use of such 'exotica' as garlic, red peppers, aubergines and olive oil. After the austerity of the postwar years this sparked a complete revolution in people's attitudes towards foods that, some forty years later, we now take for granted.

To talk glibly of a 'Mediterranean look' in design or decoration is to ignore the remarkable diversity of the region's geo- and ethnographical span. However, it is possible to draw out strong elements that occur throughout the region and that combine to create a unified and definable style.

Alphonse Daudet (1840–1897) wrote of Provence, 'born of the sun, it lives by light', and this could equally be applied to the region as a whole. Although in places the winters can be extremely cold, sunlight and heat permeate most of life in the Mediterranean. Consequently, the desire to create cool and shady environments becomes paramount. This interplay of light and shade predominates and has a strong influence on architecture, design and decoration.

The many beauties of the Mediterranean are legendary – the scents of lavender, roses and jasmine; the brilliant colours of the sea and sky; the bougainvillea blossoming wild at the roadside; its whitewashed villages, its architectural treasures, its cuisine, and its wines. All these, and more, contribute to the wider influence of the region – the wonderful sense of warmth, light and sheer well-being that springs to mind when even the word *Mediterranean* is spoken. The evocation of this feel-good factor, intrinsic to this diverse and historic region, is what makes the Mediterranean style so appealing.

Colour

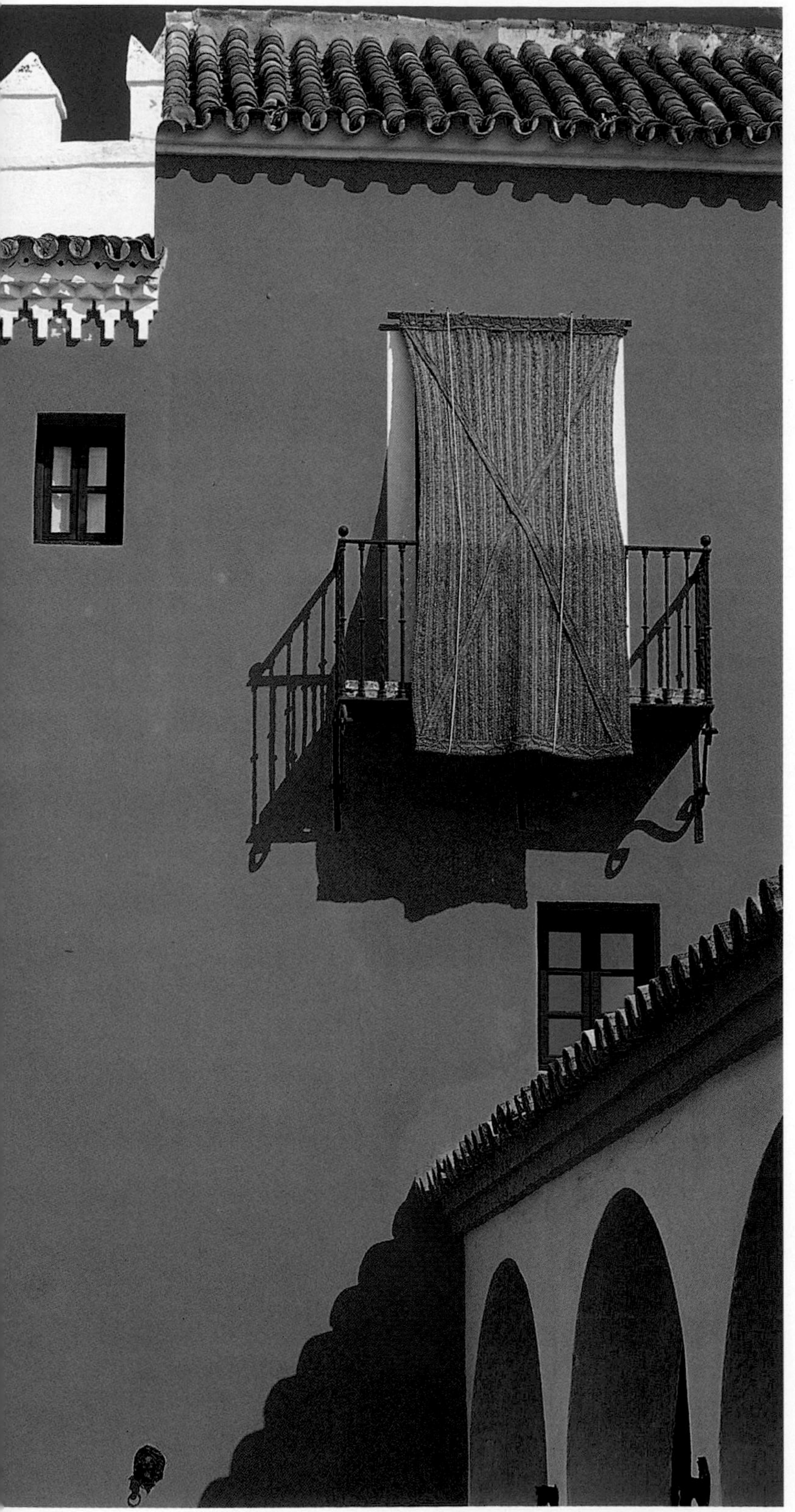

The Mediterranean palette is as rich and diverse as the natural world that inspires it. Colours draw on the infinite resources of the landscape: the azure blue of the sea and sky, the greens of cypress trees and olive groves, fields of brightly coloured flowers and, in north Africa, the rugged rocky terrain of deserts and mountains.

Mediterranean colours and combinations of colours are typically intense in hue and characterized by dramatic contrasts, again reflecting the pattern of nature. In the same way, the dusty aridity of the desert region is interspersed with lush green oases; fields of sunflowers in Tuscany glow golden against the dark green foliage; and the deep blue of the sea is edged by sandy beaches of startling whiteness. And these colours and contrasts are enhanced by a brilliance of sunlight that is virtually unknown in northern climes. Writing of Algeria, Pierre Auguste Renoir put into words the extraordinary effect this can have: 'The magic of the sun transmutes the palm trees into gold, the water seems full of diamonds and men become kings from the East'.

Three key colour schemes seem to exemplify the extraordinary richness and variety of the region. The first includes the warm reds, greens, yellows and blues as seen in the bright tones and motifs of Provençal cotton fabrics. The second is the crisp contrast of blue and white so typical of Greek island villages. And the third is the earthy palette of the north African landscape that incorporates ochre, umber, terracotta and burnt sienna. The allocation of each palette to a specific area is by no means definitive, as the various combinations interweave freely throughout the region without regard to border or boundary.

Provençal palette

Inspired by the colours and contrasts of the landscape, this palette is characterized by the bold tones of red, green and blue that come together, in man-made form, in the cotton fabrics of the region. Made famous by the 'Souleiado' name, these fabrics with their colourful floral and paisley motifs are woven and printed in the traditional manner and capture all the light and colour of the region.

Reds vary here from the deep terracotta of tiled floors through the rich, blackcurrant glow of the local wines. Many of the houses are covered with *crepi*, a render plaster finish, which weathers to a warm pinky-red over the years; and summer sees crops of bright geraniums blossoming forth from terracotta pots. As in nature, these reds are often offset by green; sage-coloured shutters and woodwork provide them with a contrasting backdrop. Bright and bold, nature's red is a strong statement: the bright flower drawing bees to its nectar; the bold plumage of the male bird out to attract a mate. Sometimes, it signals danger: red berries against dark green leaves. The national flower of Spain is the scarlet carnation, its bright petals signifying passion and beauty, the colour of the matador's cape and the bull's blood.

Provençal yellows are steeped in sunlight, from the brilliant gold of a field of sunflowers to the bright citrus-yellow of lemons. Fabrics display a yellow so deep and rich it is almost gold, and house walls painted yellow glow with a vibrancy so intense that you can hardly look at them in the midday sun.

The greens of this palette are drawn from the darkest – almost black – green of the local cypress trees through the weathered silver-grey of the olive groves. Vineyards cover the hillsides with their leafy green tendrils and the fertile soil

Above *Typical of the palette of Provence, rich red walls are offset by the soft grey-blue of the armoire and chair and the brilliant sky-blue of the open door. The chair seat is covered with a traditional Provençal quilted cotton.*

Facing *Mediterranean colours are bold and vibrant. This 11th-century Andalusian* cortijo, *or farmhouse, has been painted in a traditional yellow, called alvero, which constrasts strikingly with the blue sky beyond.*

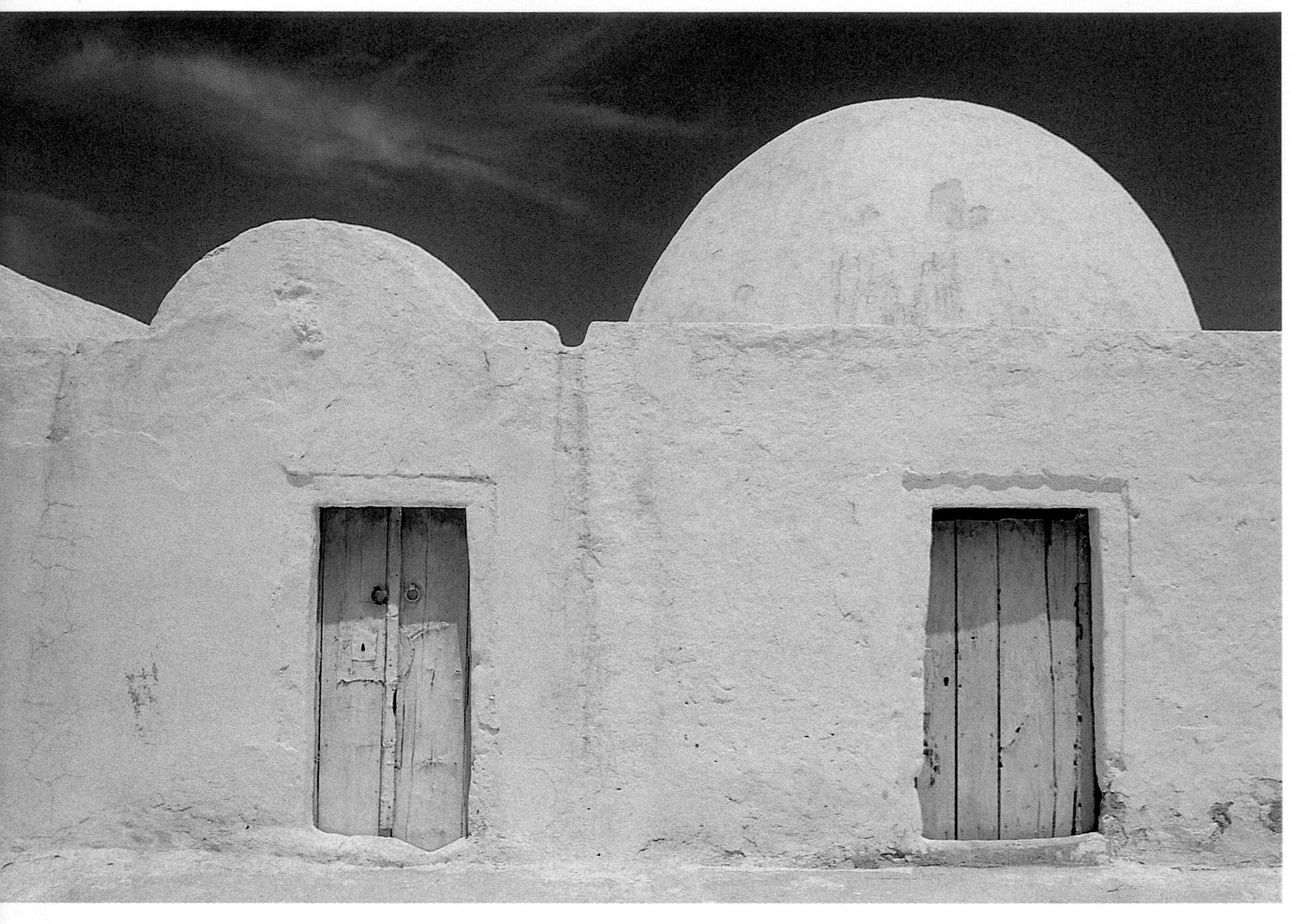

Above *The dazzlingly white walls characteristic of Greek island houses and coastal villages all around the Mediterranean are maintained by layer upon layer of limewash, applied regularly every spring.*

Facing *Doors and windows are typically painted a vivid blue, ranging from this brilliant turquoise through softer, more weathered hues (above) that have seen the passage of many seasons.*

produces crops of pale green melons, artichokes, salads and herbs. Traditionally, green is the holy colour of Islam. It symbolizes the verdant shade of the oasis, a haven for the peoples of the desert. For many cultures green is the colour of fertility and regeneration, representing the natural cycle of life and death.

Considered in the past to be the colour of the firmament overhead, the spectrum of blue in nature has an extraordinary variety and depth. Very much a key colour throughout the Mediterranean, the blue of the Provençal palette ranges from the brilliant cobalt of the sea to the azure intensity of the sky, and from the palest blue of the distant Alps to the deep violet of the lavender fields in full bloom. The colour of the sky can vary from a luminous aquamarine to the inky blue-black of night. The sea, too, is ever-changing as it reflects the brightness of the air and sky – at times a livid purple-blue, at others a brilliant turquoise.

GREEK PALETTE

The combination of blue and white is one of the most timeless in the history of decorating. It has been employed for centuries in interiors of many different styles, but the particular contrast of brilliant white and electric blue is instantly evocative of the Mediterranean. It characterizes coastal architecture from Spain and Morocco but seems at its most intense in the eastern Mediterranean: village after village in Greece seems to take as its inspiration the blue and white of the sea and sky. The houses appear ever more dazzlingly white with each annual coat of limewash, while architectural details – such as shutters, doors and window frames – are often defined in brilliant blue, and plain expanses of white wall are sometimes simply outlined or bordered in this contrasting hue. Even when its original brilliance has been bleached by the sun, this blue remains intense and the contrast is bright, bold and dramatic.

The same theme is repeated elsewhere: on the beaches there are blue deck chairs on white sand; in the streets there are blue-and-white striped café awnings; and on the water itself blue boats with white sails roll lazily on the swell while an occasional seagull bobs on the crest of an azure wave. The local fishing boats, however, are brightly painted in bold primary colours that are renewed year after year as the salt and sun take their toll. Blue and white is a typical combination but the effect lies almost as much in the degree of contrast as in the choice of palette.

Here, as elsewhere in the Mediterranean, the use of colour is bright and bold, free and easy, with none of the subtle modulations of shade or careful matchmaking and co-ordinating that usually accompanies decorating decisions in cooler climates.

In general, the simpler the architecture, the bolder the use of colour, with walls, doors, window frames, shutters, verandahs and balconies all becoming part of the canvas. The strength of the sun lends a new perspective to the choice of colours. Pastel tones with little contrast simply fade to nothing in the intense light. Bright colours and bold contrasts work best and throughout the Mediterranean colour is used for its own sake, contrasting joyously, adding life and intensity to every surface.

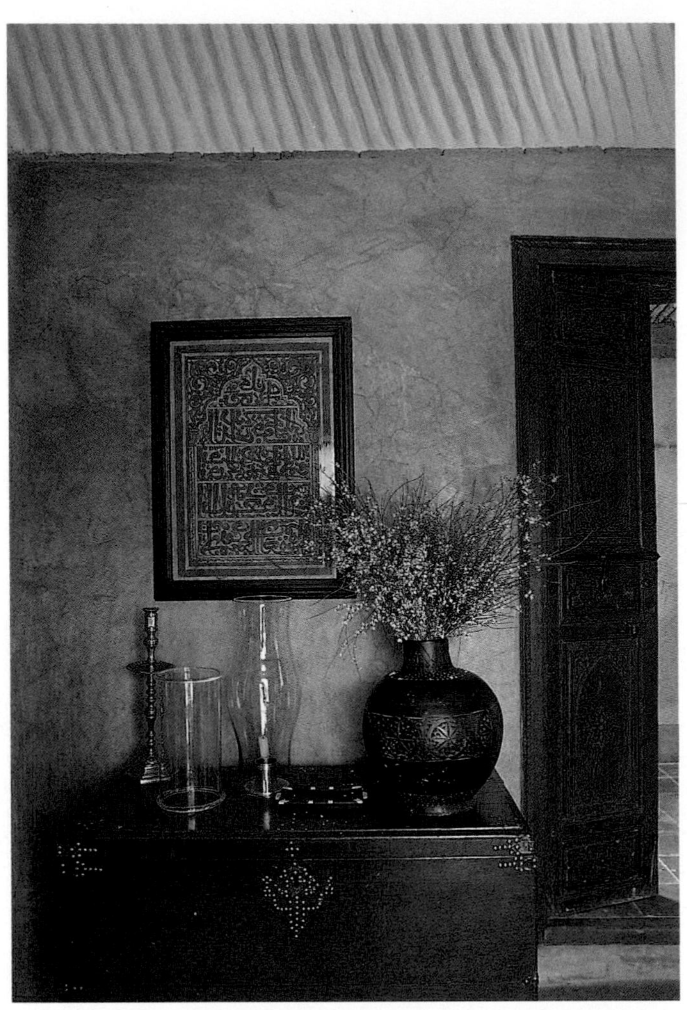

Above *An interior illustrating the warmth and richness of the north African palette combines natural woods, shining gold and brass, warm terracotta tiles and earthy pigments.*

Facing *The soil and sand tones of the north African palette are drawn from the landscape itself: the colour of the exterior wall here blends seamlessly with the unfaced rugged rock wall in the background.*

African palette

Not only has nature inspired the Mediterranean palette, it has also, until the last century, been the only source of the colours themselves. Natural dyes and pigments all came directly or indirectly from the earth: ochre, umber and sienna were obtained from clay; madder and indigo from plants; and cochineal from crushed beetles. The great nineteenth-century romantic artist Eugène Delacroix once said, 'Give me mud and I will paint the skin of Venus.' It is mud that, effectively, characterizes the tones of the African palette, and the picture it is used to paint is indeed captivatingly beautiful.

These colours are drawn from the natural tones of the often rugged landscape – the rocky terrain of the Atlas mountains, the desert sands of both northern and southern Africa, and the rich red-brown soil of more fertile areas like the Nile delta. Yellow ochre comes from a clay coloured by iron and is used to produce a variety of earthy yellow shades. Umber, another natural earth pigment, contains ferric oxide, lime, aluminium and manganese, and turns the warm red-brown of burnt umber when heated. The best quality umber originated, as the name implies, from Umbria in Italy, but now it comes from Cyprus and Turkey. The warm rich reddish-brown tones of burnt sienna result when raw sienna is roasted in a furnace; and Venetian red was originally obtained from earth coloured red by a high proportion of the deposit iron oxide.

Terracotta, which literally means 'cooked earth', lies at the heart of this colour palette. In shades that range right across the earthy spectrum from palest plaster-pink through dark reddish-brown, depending on the colour of the local earth, terracotta features throughout the Mediterranean. Roof tiles, floor tiles, even the *tagines*, or cooking pots, in Morocco, are made of terracotta.

Although apparently more closely related to the warm earthy tones of the African landscape than to the vivid colours that characterize the northern Mediterranean coastline, terracotta is an integral part of the whole region – from the Moorish-influenced architecture of Spain to the pantiled roofs of Italy and Greece.

The African palette also embraces the colours of the spice trade, such as the bright yellow of turmeric, the gold of saffron, and the rich browns of cinnamon and nutmeg. Some of the spices are indigenous; some were originally brought from the East. Often described as the floral equivalent of gold, saffron is particularly prized. Now, in the brief two weeks of the annual saffron harvest, Spain produces no less than half the world's total crop.

African Mediterranean colours are warm, rich and soft. They evoke the past: the golden stone of historic castle ramparts, the earthy render facing an ancient dwelling, the weathered brickwork of a courtyard cloister. Even on the dullest of days, they seem to glow with reflected light and are exceptionally easy to live with.

In conclusion, the Mediterranean palette in all its diversity is rich in both colour and contrast, and an appropriate use of colour is one of the major keys to recreating a sense of the Mediterranean in any setting. The strong combinations and tones may seem daunting at first but become more accessible and inspiring when seen in their natural context.

TEXTURE, PATTERN AND MOTIFS

Often described as a melting pot, a point where East meets West, where Islam touches the Christian world and where Europe rubs shoulders with both Africa and Asia, the Mediterranean is rich in cultural and artistic traditions. For centuries, there has been continuous cross-fertilization of design and technology, thanks both to traders and invaders. This is reflected in the art and architecture as well as in the ethnic craftwork.

Materials and motifs, patterns and prints, appear and reappear throughout the region; some common to many countries, some denoting – with pin-point accuracy – the origin of the piece in question. Wrought ironwork, ceramics, glass, wood carvings, rug and textile weaving are just some areas of craftsmanship for which the Mediterranean is renowned.

Ceramics provide a fascinating insight into the interchange of ideas and inspiration across the region. Lustreware was first developed along the banks of the Euphrates and the Tigris, and yet some very early examples have been excavated from a site near Cordoba in Spain. These pieces made the long journey west, from Baghdad, Damascus, Constantinople (now Istanbul) and Alexandria, to be traded for Spanish foodstuffs and minerals during the Arab occupation of Spain which lasted seven hundred years. Centuries later, following the decline of Moorish Spain, Islamic craftsmen migrated to Morocco and northern Africa, where they have also left their distinctive mark on the development of ceramics. It is obviously no coincidence that ceramic art remains a strong feature throughout the Mediterranean region, from the shimmering mosaics of the mosques and churches of Istanbul in the east, to the tiled interiors of the stately palaces and churches of Andalusia in the west, and the brilliantly colourful ethnic ceramics of northern Africa to the south.

Spain is also famed for its decorative metalwork. Rich deposits of gold, silver and iron ore in the north of the country led to the development of a thriving industry, which produced highly ornamental and decorative pieces: gates, window grilles, balconies, chancel screens, candelabra, firedogs, tables and chairs, as well as the distinctive ornamentation that adorns many Spanish front doors.

Spain also has an interesting tradition of wood carving, some of it again dating back to the cross-fertilization of Islamic and Christian ideas following the Moorish occupation. This created a vernacular style of architecture known as *mudejar*, which was characterized by the use of narrow red bricks

__Left__ The intensity of light heightens the contrasts between sun and shade, making the three-dimensional effect of a typical pantiled roof even more marked. There is a contrast of texture here too – between the faded paintwork of the flat wall and the multi-layered ranks of curved tiles.

__Right__ Layers of render, peeled back to the brickwork in places by the passage of time, reveal several generations of colour on a well-weathered wall.

decorated with tiles, and featured intricate woodwork. Finely coffered ceilings of indigenous chestnut wood are typical of this style and richly carved furniture is found throughout the region.

Rug and textile weaving are traditions that belong more to the countries of northern Africa and the near East. Turkey, Syria and Egypt all have long traditions of carpet making, including both knotted, or pile, carpets and woven kilims, while the Berbers brought primitive weaving techniques to northern Africa many centuries BC.

These traditions have produced a legacy of pattern and motif that is both decorative and highly symbolic and that tells a visual story to the informed viewer. Rugs and textiles often depict religious themes and the age-old battle between good and evil, and what may appear as a quirkily asymmetrical design may in fact be a deliberate avoidance of perfection as, in the weaver's view, perfection belongs only to God.

Motifs and Texture in Design

The motifs found commonly on Moroccan rugs and textiles often originate in the verses of the Koran or Arabic script. They can incorporate the numbers 3, 5, 7, 9, and their multiples, which are thought to have magic properties in the Arab world. Sometimes the numbers are arranged in 'magic squares', whereby the numbers add up to the same figure whether the row is read horizontally, vertically or diagonally. Geometric figures such as triangles, squares, crosses, eight-pointed stars, spirals, circles and diamonds are common; so too are leaf and floral motifs, abstract animal designs, and representations of the human eye and hand – traditionally believed to ward off the forces of evil. Animal symbols include fish which represent water and rain – all-important for the fertility of the earth. Birds are symbolic messengers between earth and heaven; while the lizard and salamander, as seekers of the sun, represent the soul searching for light. Snakes are

symbols of fertility and are thought to have healing powers; they can be portrayed in detail or simply by wavy or zigzag lines. Among the many other motifs found in a variety of media throughout the Mediterranean region are shells, crosses, stars and paisley patterns.

Above *Textile art: hand-woven in rich colours against a dark, indigo background, geometric patterns are interlinked in the design of this boldly textured rug.*

Facing *Ceramic art: tiles in an astonishing array of different shapes, sizes, textures, motifs and colours are combined with perfect precision in this lively and colourful design.*

In both architecture and design, texture plays a vital role; indeed the feel and visual effect of the finish is often as important as the colour in an interior scheme. And just as colour derives from nature, so textures, too, are natural and diverse. There is the roughness of brick and stone and plaster, often as evident inside as on the exterior walls of the house. Wood is often left rough-hewn in the beams of an old farmhouse. And the soft powdery finish of limewash and distemper has a natural tactile quality. In contrast, there is the smoothness of marble and ceramic tiles, cool to the touch however high the temperature outside; wood planed to perfection on a floor; and the polished sheen of a varnished colourwash. It is this constant juxtaposition of rough and smooth that highlights each texture in the overall scheme.

The bold textural combinations that result characterize every aspect of Mediterranean design and decoration, so that even the plainest interior is enlivened by its form and substance, whether it be a chalky coat of whitewash over a wall of rough-plastered rubblestone; a sand-and-paint mixture lending gritty texture to a smooth surface; pebbles embedded in a concrete floor; or terracotta tiles punctuated by smooth ceramic inlays. Similarly, at the other extreme, ornamentation, though often simple and naturalistic, can be used to create effects of great drama and intensity. Patterns draw on centuries of tradition and are strong and symbolic, whether gracing a woven rug, a cotton fabric, ethnic embroidery or a hand-painted ceramic bowl.

Creating the Look

Mediterranean style is bright, bold, colourful, simple, ethnic, textured, and is firmly underpinned by its emphasis on natural materials and natural effects. Although extraordinarily diverse in its national or regional manifestations, there is something at its core that is not only attractive and relevant to the Mediterranean itself, but has a much greater and wider appeal.

The style is founded on bold simplicity. To recreate its look does not require great skill, nor does it involve complicated techniques. It relies far more for effect on the liberal use of solid areas of colour, and texture, than on carefully contrived decorative schemes. Mediterranean style is characterized by an absence of fussiness or clutter. It is minimalism on a natural theme, where the interior is not an arty statement but a place in which simple furniture and objects seem to be intrinsic elements in an environment for essentially practical living. Floors are often left bare, perhaps with one rug or runner. Walls are simply painted and frequently left 'unpictured'. Fabric is kept to a minimum, with plain linens, calicoes, butter muslins and heavily textured woven textiles taking precedence over highly patterned and coloured designs.

There is a sense of space and light that is worlds away from the overly decorated interiors of previous decades. Rooms glow with warmth and colour and, whatever the climate outside, the sun appears to be streaming in. Natural light is always preferred to an artificial alternative, and is replaced by candlelight at night if possible and practical.

Not only do these interiors reflect the world outside, they are, ideally, oriented towards it, with outdoor areas such as terraces or patios decorated and furnished to provide a natural extension to the indoor living space.

Adapting the Style

The Mediterranean look is very much in tune with current trends in design and decoration, expressing the general desire for a less contrived, less complicated, less 'decorated' style. It is affordable and achievable, even when you are working within a limited space and with a limited budget. It favours the natural over the artificial, satisfying environmental concerns by rejecting man-made substances such as plastics and acrylics in favour of materials (preferably available locally) such as stone, wood, clay, iron and cotton. Those nostalgic for the past will find the revival of old-fashioned techniques, such as limewashing, an appealing option.

Undoubtedly, compromises will have to be made to accommodate a less favourable climate. For the many people who live in urban environments, space will be at a premium

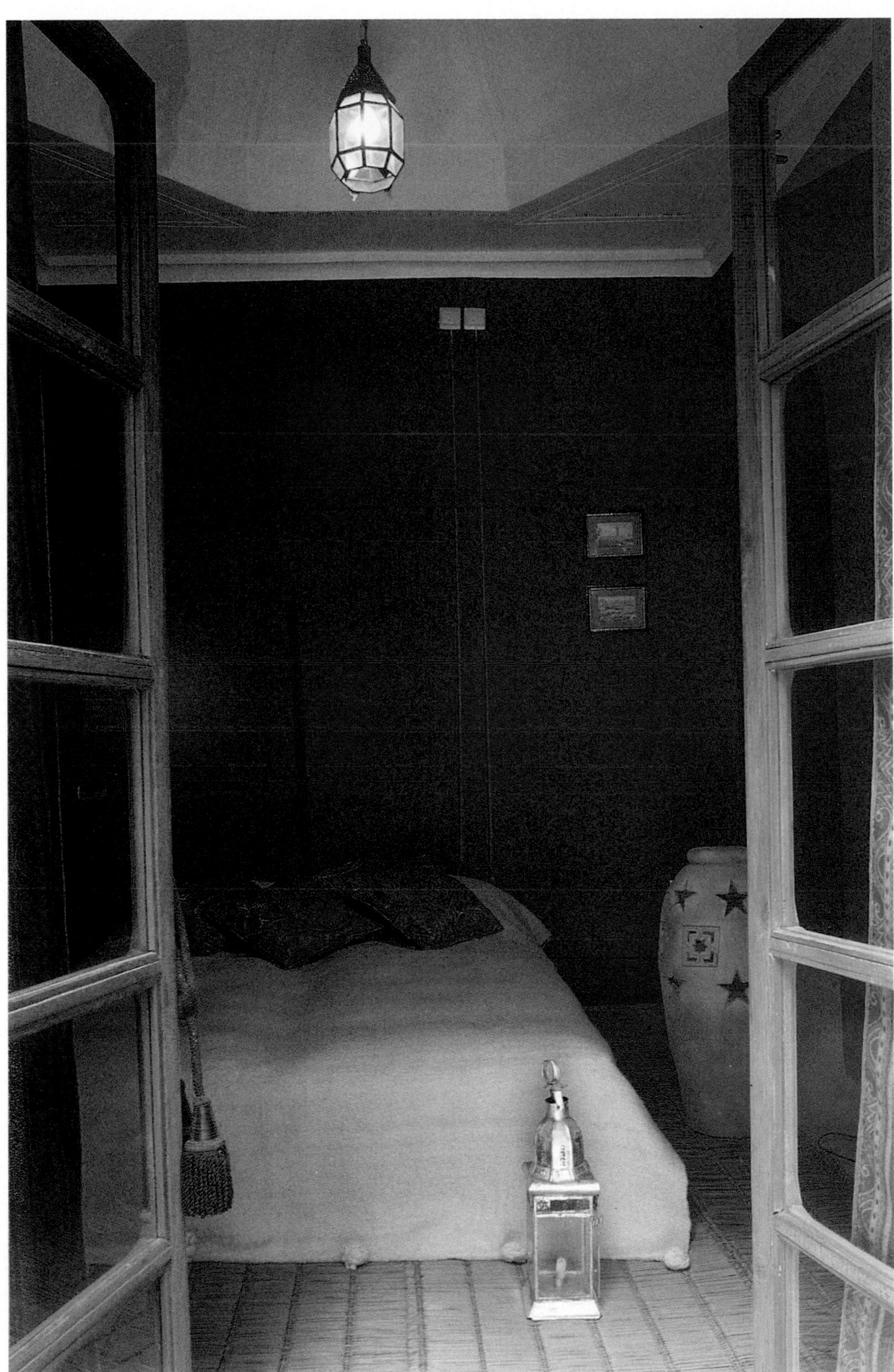

Left *Bold, bright colour is a key to Mediterranean decoration, especially when combined with appropriate furniture and furnishings. Setting off the red walls with natural flooring, lanterns, a striking terracotta jar, and some patterned cushions on the simple bed, works to create an authentic Mediterranean look.*

Facing *Walls can be transformed by the simplest paint effects. This small bathroom is brightened by the contrasting border around the cupboard door and the repeating zigzag frieze.*

and lunch on the terrace or even a drink on the balcony can be no more than a dream. However, using vibrant, glowing colours, a lush profusion of plants, and shutters at the windows, can create the impression of heat and light, with the promise of a sun-filled world outside, that is the essence of the Mediterranean interior.

The Mediterranean house is, of course, built for hot weather, with thick walls, cool flooring materials, shuttered or screened windows to diffuse the bright light, and ever-open doorways. Further from the Mediterranean in more temperate climates, houses are, by contrast, designed to generate and retain heat and maximize light. Once again, a compromise is possible, the solution lying in creating an effect rather than in the reality of the situation. Shutters can be just as draughtproof as curtains. Radiators can become less obtrusive if they are concealed under a built-in, Mediterranean-style, window seat. You can benefit from the warmth of carpeting, but it will look more authentic if you restrict yourself to rugs and runners that are more reminiscent of the Mediterranean than fitted carpets; or you can use natural floor coverings like sisal and seagrass. And by choosing furniture made out of wickerwork, wood or metal that would look just as at home in a garden as inside the house, the interior space takes on an appropriately outdoor dimension.

This book aims to define the different elements of the Mediterranean environment that combine to create its sun-drenched, carefree style; to draw together the various strands, and to give suggestions as to how these elements may be used to create an authentic Mediterranean feeling in your own home. Paul Theroux captured the magic of the region when he wrote, 'The very word Mediterranean signified sunny skies and balmy weather, and for thousands of years these shores had been a kind of Eden, fruitful with grapes and olives and lemons'. What better reason could there be to explore further?

Above *Vibrantly coloured walls and a bold, checked floor pattern are the dominant features in this kitchen, while objects that are both utilitarian and decorative are characteristically displayed on an open shelf and tabletop.*

Facing *A cupboard becomes the focus of attention, set against a simple monochrome backdrop. Painted a vivid shade of aquamarine that is entirely in keeping with the bright character of the Mediterranean, it is topped with an array of typical ceramic pots and candlesticks.*

Walls and Floors

WALLS

An emphasis on natural materials and natural textures is a recurring theme in all aspects of decoration in the Mediterreanean house, and is nowhere better illustrated than in the treatment of walls and floors.

Walls of unadorned stone are not uncommon in Mediterranean houses. With the ever-present link between interior and exterior living, interior walls inevitably tend to reflect the natural tones and textures of the world outside, and are made with the same local materials and techniques that are used to construct the outer façade.

A traditional farmhouse in Majorca or Provence, for example, might have walls of local 'rubblestone' (roughly hewn blocks of stone bonded together with thick slabs of mortar) which might be left bare inside the house, or at most roughly plastered and given a quick coat of whitewash. Far from being finished to a satiny smoothness, walls are typically left rough and ready, with their defects not artificially concealed but actively turned to advantage when decorating. Irregularities in the wall's surface – or the room's shape – are considered intrinsic to a structure; and since so much of life is spent outdoors, it is deemed unnecessary to waste time achieving meticulous perfection indoors.

Elsewhere, interior walls may be more or less smoothly plastered, but door and window architraves might be made of exposed rough-hewn stone or terracotta brickwork, which has more in common with the exterior of the house.

PAINT

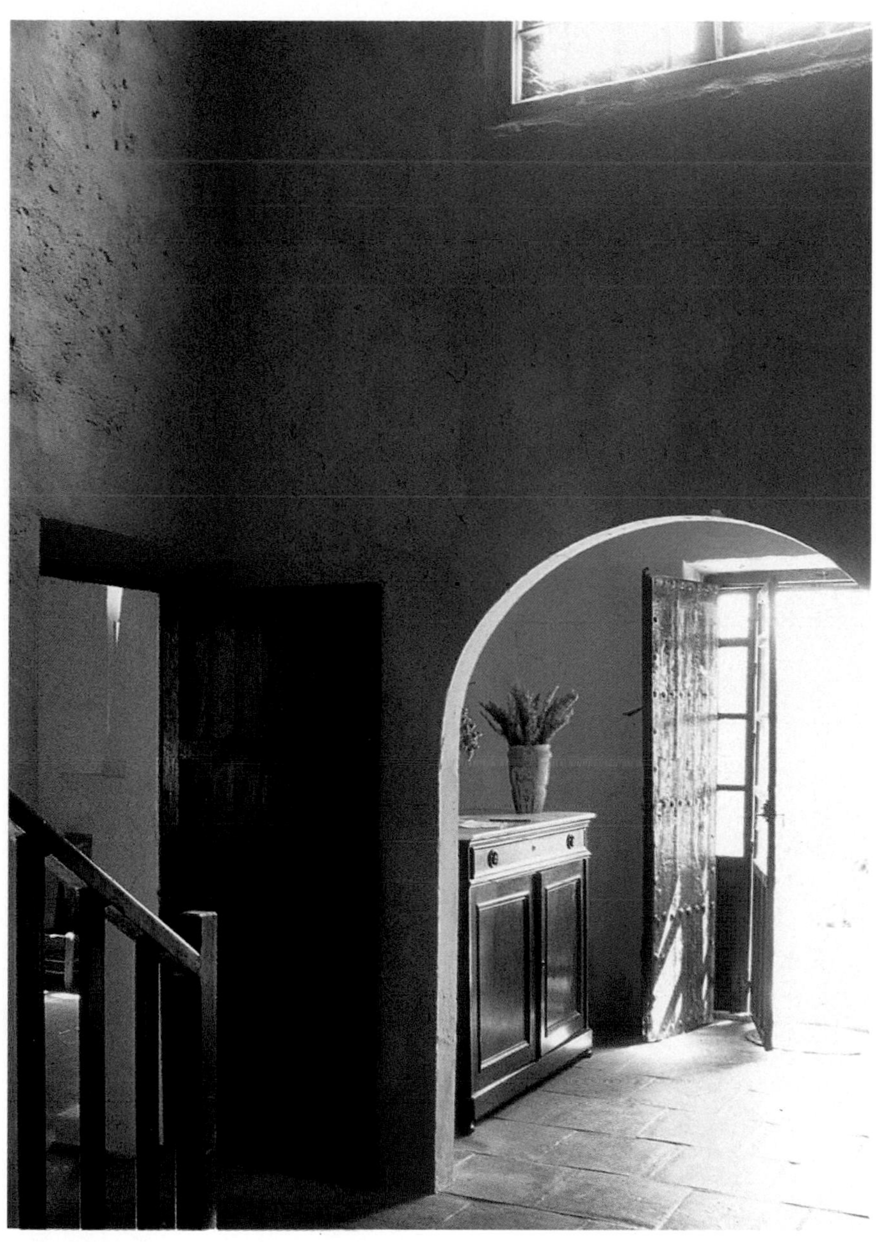

Paint is still by far the most popular and most typical Mediterranean wall finish. From the sparkling whiter-than-white whitewash of the Côte d'Azur and Greek island houses, right through the spectrum via the ice-cream pastels of the Italian Riviera, to the finely executed and richly coloured frescoes of historic palaces across the region – the range and versatility of the paints and paint effects are enormous. Using natural pigments, manufactured by using time-honoured methods, these paints blend harmoniously with their surroundings both in texture and tone. Traditional paints such as whitewash and distemper feature strongly. The colour palette is rich, ranging from the earthy tones of terracotta, saffron and *sang de boeuf*, to sky blue, lime green, and yellow.

Much of the Mediterranean character, and the beauty of these colours as seen in situ, lie in the effects achieved not just by the artist/craftsman but by the hand of nature. Seasons of brilliant sunshine soften and bleach the originally vivid tones and naturally 'distress' them to give a patina that we can only aspire to emulate. Colourwashes, rubbed paint finishes and certain varnishes can all help to achieve this faded and evocative look.

Simplicity is always the key. Colour is used in bold planes, drawing together and defining spaces within open-plan areas of the house as well as outside. Contrasting colour is used to create interest: a painted cornice-level border or chair rail, for example, or an outline around a structural arch, doorway or cupboard to emphasize a feature or architectural detail.

Above *Bold colours are freely juxtaposed here, the warm, earthy red of the staircase hall giving way to sky blue in the entrance, offering a cool respite from the heat of the day outside.*

Facing *Broad stripes in a trio of colours enliven the walls and archways of this passage, while more ornamental decoration around and above the window makes it a strong focal point.*

WHITEWASH

Many Mediterranean painted walls, both inside and out, look powdery or chalky and give the impression that paint dust will rub off on your clothes or hands should you brush against them. This soft, ultra-matt finish cannot be achieved using the standard two coats of conventional matt emulsion but is usually associated with the more old-fashioned paints such as whitewash, and its two variants, distemper and limewash, which are now enjoying a new popularity, having been overshadowed for some time by more modern, technologically more 'advanced' paints.

These paints, and the techniques used to apply them, have evolved over several centuries. Traditionally, the exteriors of buildings were limewashed, while the interiors were coated with distemper. They were – and are – cheap to produce, they could be tinted if required, and they were easy to apply. Today, village after village around the Mediterranean coastline is still revitalized every spring by a coat of whitewash or limewash. Although this simple annual coat of paint serves to enhance the intrinsically picturesque architecture of the towns, it also has a very practical purpose. Limewash, suitable for exterior use, is used to cover up any damage done by the elements over the winter, as well as any general defects such as damp patches that might appear on the façade. It was also believed to counter the extreme heat of summer and keep away the flies.

As both distemper and limewash are water-based, they are absorbed into a wall's surface and allow it to 'breathe' naturally. Thus, water and salts from the wall are able to pass through the layer of paint rather than becoming trapped within it, which can cause peeling or cracking, particularly with new plaster. Distemper is particularly suitable for use on uneven surfaces as the matt finish does not catch the light and thus camouflages any lumps rather than highlighting them.

Distemper comprises pigments, whiting (crushed chalk), glue size and water; limewash uses slaked lime instead of

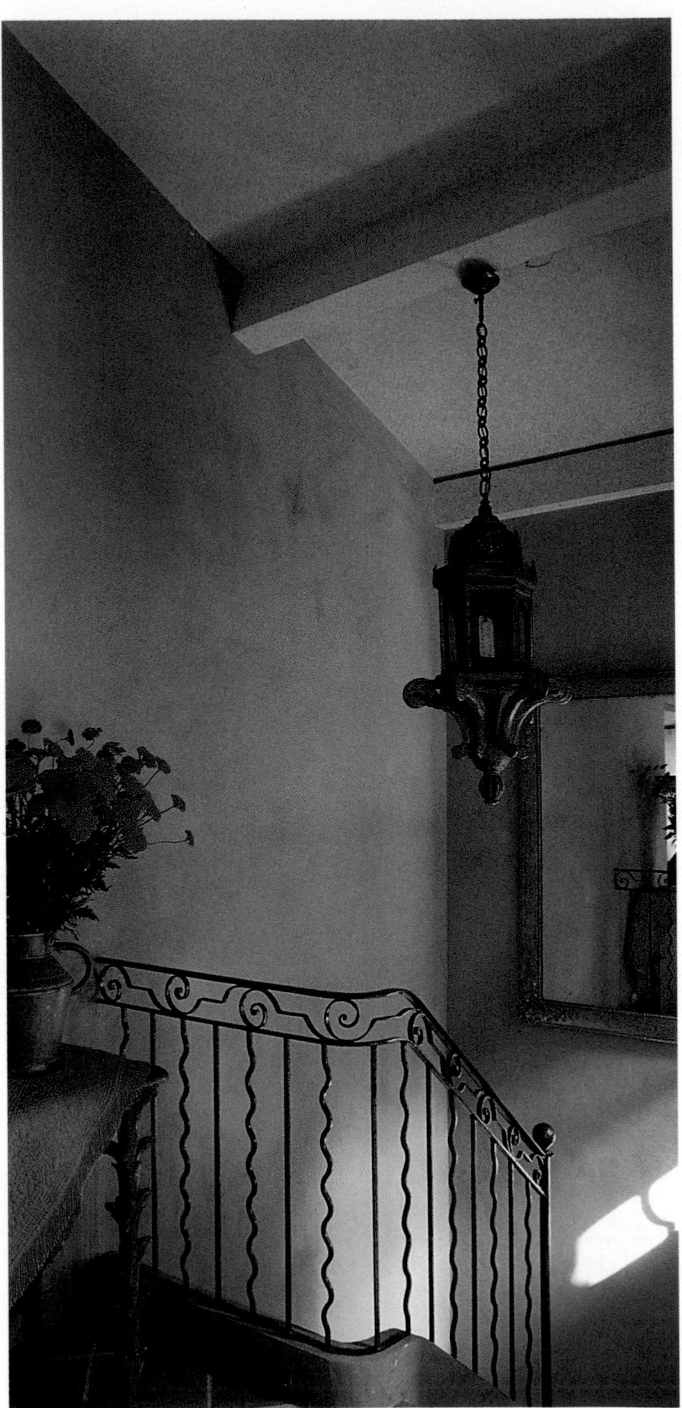

Above *Powdery blue paint lends colour and depth to a stairwell. The matt finish softens any surface irregularities in the plaster.*

whiting; and oil-bound distemper, a third variant, has an emulsion of oil and water as a binder. All three whitewashes achieve a matt, powdery texture. Although not generally on sale in home improvement stores, these paints are increasingly available from specialist paint suppliers. Limewash is highly toxic, but the recipe for distemper is straightforward, so you can make your own. Be warned, however: distemper only keeps for a day or two, so only mix what you need for immediate use; it also dries very quickly as you apply it, but a tablespoonful of glycerine per litre (quart) of paint will lengthen the drying time allowing for a smoother, more regular finish.

It can be applied successfully over existing emulsion paint, provided it is clean, grease-free and dry, but existing distemper must be entirely removed. To do this, scrub down the surface of the wall with a dry brush to remove any loose flakes and then, using plenty of warm water, scrub hard with a stiff brush. Change the water as it becomes milky and, once it remains clear and all traces of the old distemper have gone, rinse the wall with clean water and dry it with a soft cloth or sponge. Leave it to dry out, then apply a base coat of primer, sealer or undercoat. Depending upon the surface of the walls and upon the effect required, a room may take as little as one coat of distemper or as many as three. Avoid using a final coat of varnish as this will detract from the soft, delicate finish.

It is possible to imitate, to a degree, the effect of real distemper by using standard over-the-counter paints. One method is to apply a 'wash' of matt, water-based emulsion, thinned with water, over a flat emulsion base coat or coats. The effect will be wonderfully matt but will lack the soft powdery texture of true distemper. However, you will need to experiment first, as the finished effect will depend on a variety of factors, such as the state and age of the plaster and how many layers of paint there are on the wall already. Use test squares of hardboard or cardboard to check the effect if you do not want to try it on the wall itself.

Above *Layers of chalky white paint, recoated every year, blanket a tunnel-like staircase, creating unity and harmony by drawing together the uneven surfaces of the walls and floor.*

COLOURWASHES

Colour is just as typical of the Mediterranean as is the sparkling white of many of the coastal villages. Both internal and external walls reflect the many natural pigments traditionally used to colour their surfaces: burnt umber, raw and burnt sienna, Venetian red and yellow ochre, to name but a few. Colour is applied in various forms. In Provence, the *crepi*, a coloured plaster, weathers gently over the years to a rusty red and warm geranium pink. In Italy and parts of Spain, such plasters come in paler shades of cream, stone, pink and cantaloupe. Pigments are added to limewash for exterior walls, and to distemper, its interior counterpart.

These traditional paints adapt particularly well to techniques such as colourwashing, which is simply the application of a thin layer of colour over a painted ground of a different colour or tone. Such a technique is perfect for the uneven, irregular walls of simple Mediterranean houses on which a flat colour would tend to emphasize any defects in the surface. Colourwashes can be applied very lightly to give an almost translucent effect or, alternatively, can be built up, layer upon layer, to create a vivid intensity of colour. Colourwashes can be applied with a brush or cloth and can be even or patchy in effect, depending on the surface underneath and the amount of paint applied. With a colourwash, even the smoothest of modern walls can be given something of the character and rich patina of colour so typical of Mediterranean houses. It is always wise to test the effect in a concealed corner before embarking on a whole wall.

Repainting a house is probably the easiest way to give it a facelift, and dramatic results can be achieved with minimal outlay. It may even be possible to use existing paintwork as a base for a colourwash. Wash the wall first to remove accumulated grime: ammonia, sugar soap (alkaline compound), or vinegar in warm water should have the desired effect.

Coloured distemper, applied normally, gives a flat, matt finish, but for colourwashing it needs to be thinned with water to the consistency of milk. Alternatively, use thinned-down emulsion paint or simply combine water, tinted with gouache colour (one small tube to half a litre [one pint] of water), with a dollop of emulsion paint to give it some body. It is best to apply a wash over a flat emulsion ground, which is more absorbent than an oil-based undercoat. Unlike an oil glaze, which takes some time to dry, emulsion dries quickly, leaving a less even effect and a more chalky texture. Most emulsion washes benefit from being protected by one or two coats of matt varnish; this will ensure that they last longer, whilst not spoiling their airy luminous effect.

Above *Vibrant use of colour transforms a plain wall. The flowers in the niche echo the rich tones of the colourwash that vary with the intensity of light from vivid orange at the base to brilliant saffron higher up.*

Facing *A bold blue colourwash on the walls, between the rafters of the ceiling and on the woodwork of the doors and windows, creates a dramatic backdrop for a day bed.*

Above *Clearly visible beneath the top coat of white paint, the construction of this wall from lumps of rough stone bonded together with mortar adds a certain texture and life to the simplicity of this interior.*

Facing *Subtle variations of colour and texture in the paint finish on this plain plastered wall make it a sympathetic partner to the rustic wooden beams and 'distressed' pine dresser.*

Plaster and paint textures

The use of textured plaster and paint seems to follow naturally from the widespread popularity of untreated wood, brick and stone. The textured paint effects achieved by using distemper and colourwashes are visible only to the eye, but both paint and plaster can also be textured to the touch.

Plaster can be applied in a relatively thin layer over walls of rough-hewn stone or brick to create a smoother finish while retaining the tactile quality of the materials beneath. It can also be applied in a textured form by being built up on the wall in layers thick enough to be scored with linear or abstract patterns, or simply left rough, flicked up rather than smoothed down by the plasterer's trowel. For a completely natural look, it can simply be left bare, sealed only with a coat of matt varnish.

Paint can be applied to emphasize these plaster patterns or, alternatively, to add a texture of its own. An authentically gritty texture reminiscent of rough, sandstone walls can be achieved merely by mixing handfuls of fine sand into standard emulsion paint (see pages 36–37). Existing paintwork can easily be given a textured or 'distressed' look by the 'artistic' use of sandpaper and a variety of scraping tools. However, the success of the finished effect will depend on whether the colours are appropriate and the scraping away does not just reveal layers of old wallpaper.

The arts of plastering and painting came together most significantly in the Mediterranean in the exquisite frescoes of the Renaissance (c. 15–16th centuries AD). Literally meaning 'fresh', the fresco technique involves applying a mixture of pure pigment and lime water to freshly applied plaster while it is still wet. Absorbed into the plaster as it dries, the paint reacts with carbon dioxide in the air to form a hard, permanent surface and vivid colours of extraordinary translucence. Frescoes are still created today, but more often the technique is employed by expert conservation officers working on major restoration projects in churches, villas and palazzos.

It is possible to achieve similar effects on a humbler scale in your own home. The key is to create a 'thirsty' surface that will take up and absorb the colour as it dries. Use a standard filler, mixed as per instructions to a creamy consistency, and spread it thinly over the wall, working quickly in order to achieve a smooth, even surface. Colour is used in the form of powder, gouache or acrylic paint mixed with water, and applied before the filler dries. A thin coat of soft white wax gives the final touch; this should be burnished lightly with a cloth to bring out the colours.

A simpler method, which can achieve a similar effect, is to rub colour on to, or off, a dry base colour. The best emulsion for an effective undercoat is a standard vinyl silk emulsion (satin-finish latex). Once the undercoat has been applied to the wall, dab a mixture of oil glaze and white spirit (in a 1:3 ratio) over the top. This should be tinted with stainers or colours for the desired effect. Add a spoonful of matt white paint per 0.5 litre (one pint) of mixture. Use rags to spread the colour, or build up the intensity in layers until the desired effect is achieved. Once again, a coat or two of varnish will help to seal and protect the surface.

Tools & Materials

- Water-based paint (concentrated or standard emulsion)
- Grit or sand
- Length of muslin
- Colander or sieve
- Sugar soap and water
- Bucket
- Paint tray and roller
- Large (10 cm/4 in) paintbrush

Decide on the effect you want; this will vary according to the size of grit you are using. Grit is available in different grades from home improvement stores and some garden centres. Do not use pieces larger than 1 mm ($\frac{1}{20}$ in). For a lighter effect, sand can be used. Because the paint is to be mixed with grit, twice the usual amount will be needed to cover the wall.

Method

- Prepare the grit for mixing. Remove any dirt by placing the grit in muslin and rinsing well under a hose. Spread it out on a flat surface and allow to dry. Then sift out the larger stones using a colander or garden sieve **1**.
- The walls should be clean and smooth. Wash them with a solution of sugar soap (alkaline compound) and water, and allow 24 hours for them to dry.
- If using a concentrated paint that needs to be thinned with a little water, pour it into a bucket and stir well.

Sand-textured Walls

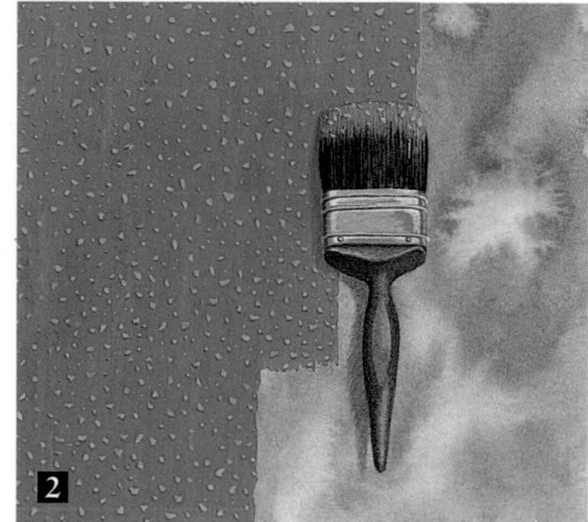

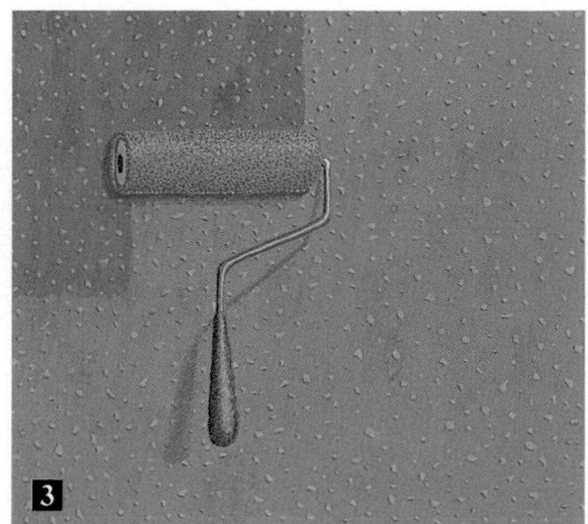

● Prepare the mixture in small batches so that the grit is evenly distributed. Use one-part grit to one-part paint, and pour it, batch by batch, into a paint tray. This prevents the grit from sinking to the bottom. You must remember to save enough paint, without grit in it, to apply a second coat.

● Working quickly, apply the paint/grit base coat using a large paintbrush **2**. Work from the top to the bottom of the wall, covering a small area at a time and applying the paint thickly so that the grit sticks to the wall.

● When the first coat has dried (usually after about four hours), apply the second coat using ungritted paint, this time with a roller **3**. Start with an upward stroke and work in all directions so that the paint is evenly distributed. Experiment with the direction of your strokes to enhance the rough texture of the wall.

Always work in a well-ventilated space when painting large areas.

Left *Textured paint takes on a new dimension in this vaulted sitting room: the abstract patterns on the wall have been created by systematically scraping off the textured mixture before it dries.*

TILE VARIATIONS

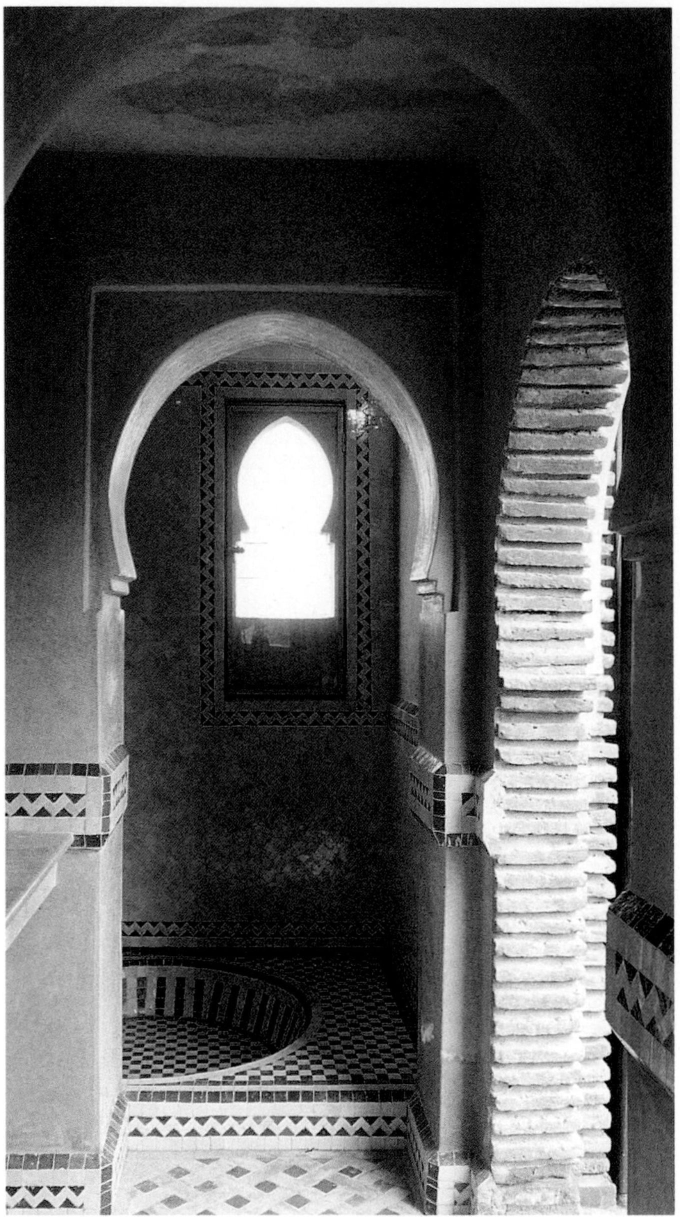

Above *Picking up the colours and patterns used in the shower recess, tiled skirting boards and dado embellish otherwise plain, plastered walls. The motif is also used around the keyhole window.*

Facing *A lozenge pattern of small, colourful tiles is used here not only for splashback and work surface but also to line the basin and to create an ornamental surround for the inset mirror.*

TILES

The long tradition of ceramic tile making around the Mediterranean is as strong today as it has always been. Italian craftsmen, for example, have been producing ceramic tiles since the Middle Ages and Italy remains the largest manufacturer of ceramic tiles in the world.

By the thirteenth century there was a thriving industry in Spain, producing the traditional *azulejos*, brightly glazed tiles, that are so typical of historic Spanish houses. Migrant Persian potters set themselves up in Malaga but the industry later spread to the area around Valencia. *Azulejos* were used on patios and courtyards, for skirting boards, dadoes and, in certain notable cases, they were used to tile complete walls, floors and staircases. They were also used for street signs, commemoration plaques and altar fonts. In the south of Spain particularly, floors were and still are invariably tiled with large square terracotta tiles that are made from clay and crushed almond husks and left out in the sun to dry. They are often laid in combination with decorative tiles.

The town of Fez is the major centre of ceramic production in Morocco and here, too, the tradition goes back for many centuries. As the Moorish Empire declined in Spain, craftsmen migrated southwards bringing new techniques and that had a great impact on indigenous artisans. Brightly painted and glazed ceramic tiles were and are used extensively for decorative purposes on floors, walls and even rooftops.

Cool both to the eye and to the touch, ceramic tiles are ideal for walls and floors in hot climates and are also relatively cheap to make. There is an infinite variety of styles and designs and plain and patterned tiles can be combined to advantage, not least in order to reduce the overall cost.

Even plain terracotta varies in colour, from dark, orangey brown right through to pale almost pink. While the darker shades might be more suitable for areas of intensive use such as passages or hallways, the paler varieties might be more appropriate in a living room. Standard squares of either terracotta or glazed colour can be given a new dimension by being laid on the diagonal, running across the room from corner to corner rather than straight from wall to wall. And tiles that are handmade, rather than machine-made, have an attractive irregularity of shape, texture and colour that is typical of the Mediterranean look.

Outside the region, tiling entire walls and floors tends to be restricted to the more functional areas such as kitchens and bathrooms, but one glance at the decorative use of tiles in Spain is enough to demonstrate how much more potential there is for tiling. In Spanish houses, room after room reveals tiling of breathtaking colour and excitement. Murals of geometric or pictorial design, more often than not a combination of the two, seem to dance across the walls, creating interiors that are cool to the touch as well as being vibrantly warm and rich visually. Such rooms need no more than a plain tiled or wooden floor and minimal furnishing to look complete.

Simply using different sizes of tile is enough to create very diverse effects. Reminiscent of Roman floors excavated at sites such as Pompeii and at Agrigento in Sicily, tiny mosaic squares can be used to create exceptionally fluid geometric or pictorial designs. They can be used alone or as a contrasting border around a

Left *The exuberant blue-and-white tiling of the walls is divided from the more sober checked floor by a border of plain, dark tiles.*

Facing *Multicoloured and multi-patterned tiles cover every surface, incorporating a variety of flower and leaf motifs and, in the foreground, a disconcertingly three-dimensional effect.*

conventionally tiled area. Standard square 10 cm (4 in) or 15 cm (6 in) tiles serve a useful purpose in kitchens and bathrooms but it is worth searching out larger sizes for a more dramatic impact. A small room will even appear to be more spacious if the proportions of the tiling are scaled up.

Tiling smaller areas

Tiling is an art form in the Mediterranean, and tiled pictures have developed as a more accessible form of the tiled murals of Spain. Designed to be set into a wall of plain tiles, these comprise a rectangular panel of tiles put together to form a picture or design within a decorative 'frame'. This idea can be adapted to be set into a plastered wall or, alternatively, framed in wood and hung as a conventional picture.

The practical nature of ceramic tiles makes them ideal for use around hobs and sinks in the kitchen, and around baths and showers in the bathroom, although here too their enormous decorative potential should always be exploited if these rooms are to look really Mediterranean; they need not be dull just because their purpose is functional. Simply choosing an appropriately Mediterranean colour such as deep aquamarine or bright lemony yellow will instantly introduce warmth and life to such areas. Combining two colours in a geometric pattern or insetting contrasting plain or patterned tiles at intervals can add vitality to any essentially practical surface. It is possible to commission tiles with a motif or design that has some special significance for you; heraldic designs, for example, were popular in sixteenth-century Spain.

Mosaic tiles lend themselves well to use in smaller areas, their size making them relatively easy to fit in awkward corners or on curved surfaces. They can be fashioned into decorative splashbacks and worktops or used to create patterned edging. Glazed tiles are non-porous and, in mosaic form, they can even be used to line a sink, allowing the pattern and colour of the surrounding tiling to continue uninterrupted for maximum decorative effect (see page 39). Take care when moulding the shape of the sink. Make it deep enough to be practical and ensure that the drainage hole is at the lowest point, otherwise a constant pool of water will form around the hole and cause unsightly build up. Use a mosaic of tiles of one colour, with same or contrasting coloured grout, or combine tiles of different colours.

The easy availability of tiles almost everywhere in the Mediterranean has led to the development of many ingenious ways of using them. For example, cutting or breaking standard square tiles and laying them in abstract mosaics of colour and pattern is an old technique that can be used to bring a new dimension to the inside of a shower or to a kitchen worktop. A traditional form of this art called *zillij* was centred in Fez and was at its height between the twelfth and fifteenth centuries. In its earlier forms, monochrome tiles were cut and rearranged into geometric patterns but, later, curvilinear and rectangular pieces in many colours were cut from large glazed panels and reassembled into ornate patterns that often incorporated Islamic motifs. Examples can still be seen decorating the floors, dadoes, columns and fountains in many of Morocco's mosques and private houses.

TILED BORDERS

The basic simplicity so typical of houses in the Mediterranean is often enlivened by a single colourful touch in the form of decorative tiled borders. Patterned with flamboyant motifs or glazed in characteristically bold plain colours, they are a versatile and inexpensive way of adding interest to tiled and painted walls alike.

At the grander end of the scale, on the tiled walls in larger Mediterranean homes, border tiles are used to simulate the effect of panelling. Typically, they are used to frame tiled murals but could just as easily be adapted to lend life to a wall of plain tiles. They also appear in place of the conventional wooden dado rail, usually bordering a tiled dado below and

often echoing its design. This might serve a practical purpose in a tiled bathroom or shower but could also be used to create decorative detail in a non-tiled room simply by setting the tiles into the plastered wall and painting the surrounding surfaces.

Equally, tiled borders can be used extensively in the utilitarian areas of the house, edging a kitchen worktop with a contrasting colour or defining a bath or basin splashback in a co-ordinating pattern. Tiles of appropriately Mediterranean colours and patterns are widely available.

Many Spanish houses, both old and new, have floor-level tiles. These are made up of plain or patterned tiles, used in classic square or rectangular forms or cut and laid on the diagonal to create a zigzag effect. They are used both on tiled and painted walls, sometimes repeating a border of patterned tiles that decorates a plain tiled floor. Either way, the result is both pretty and practical and, because glazed ceramics in this situation are as tough, if not tougher, than painted wood, they would certainly withstand moisture and general wear and tear just as effectively.

Patterned tiles are typically also laid on stair risers in Spain, Italy and Provence. Ingeniously making decorative use of the part of the staircase that is often seen from the hall or living room, this can transform the simplest, most rustic setting by creating an upward sweep of colour and pattern. As well as being attractive and easy to clean, a ceramic surface on stairs is ideal; the constant passage of feet and the accompanying scuffing will have little effect on the high glaze.

Above *Running all around the top of the walls, this bold blue-and-white border is used to divide the tiled shower area of the bathroom from the rest of the room.*

Facing *Bold tiles in jewel-like colours not only make a striking feature of this staircase, they also serve to alleviate the tunnel-like effect of the enclosed stairwell.*

Tools & Materials

- Metal ruler
- Tile cutter or scorer and matchstick
- Rough sandpaper or carborundum file
- Tile adhesive and spreader
- Grout and round-tipped stick
- Spatula and cloth

The surface to be tiled must be clean, dry and even. If you are tiling around the edge of a bath, use waterproof grout and adhesive. If working near a fireplace, use heat-resistant tiles. Coloured grout is also available if desired.

Method

- Measure the width of your wall. Divide this by the width of one repeat of your border pattern in order to calculate the number of repeats in your border (and hence the number of tiles required). Adjust the pattern if necessary to make the repeats fit symmetrically at either end of the wall. Tiles can later be cut to size using a tile cutter.
- Working with a metal ruler, score cutting lines on the undersides of each tile and cut them to size as required. We used a 'score and snap' tile cutter **1**. Alternatively, break the tiles along the scored line by placing a matchstick under the line and pressing hard on either side.

In our example, all the tiles in the border were first reduced in size, but kept

TILED BORDERS

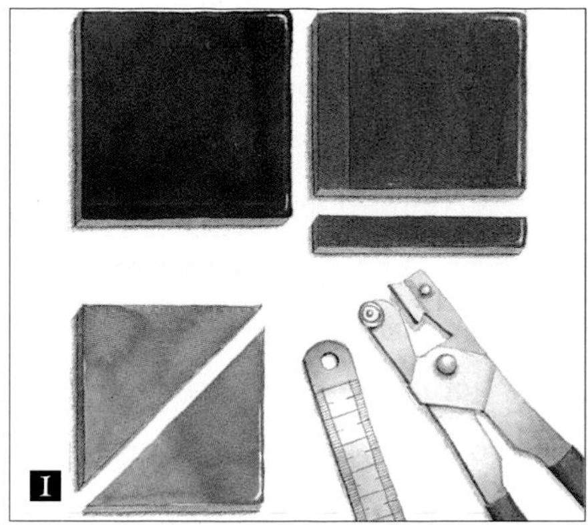

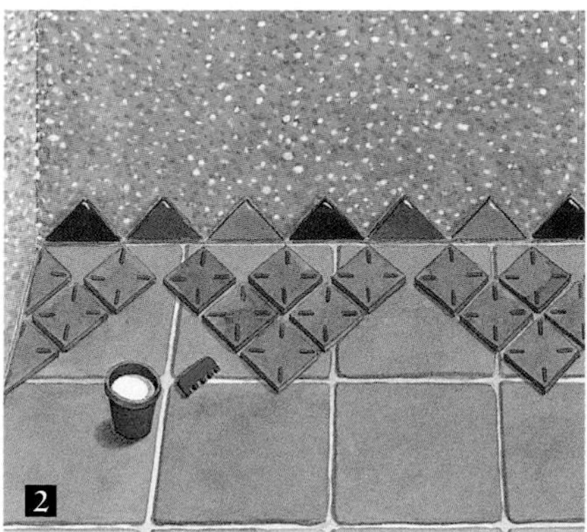

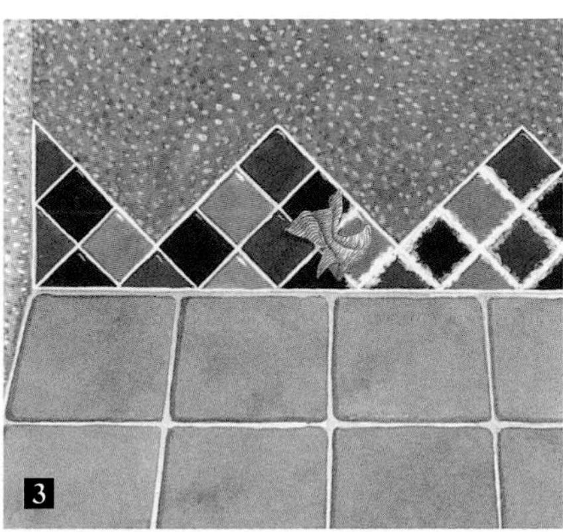

square by cutting along two adjacent edges. Those tiles forming the base of the border were then cut diagonally.

- Sand cut edges to make them smooth.
- Build up and check the border pattern by laying the tiles right side up on the floor along the wall **2**. Leave enough space between the tiles as if for the grout.
- Begin to fix the border to the wall by applying tile adhesive to the backs of the tiles with a spreader. Build the design upwards from the bottom row and leave grouting space between the tiles as you press them onto the wall. When the border is completed, leave for 24 hours to allow the adhesive to dry.
- Apply the grout using a spatula or a dry cloth. Push the grout down between the tiles and finish off by running a round-tipped stick along the line of grout. Clean the excess grout from the tiles with a damp cloth and leave to dry for a few hours **3**.

Finally, apply a layer of grout along the top edge of the border. Smooth and allow to dry before again removing the excess with a damp cloth. Polish the tiles with a dry cloth.

If you have sensitive skin, be sure to wear rubber gloves while grouting.

Left *Pentagonal tiles create a decorative floor-level border, the zigzag edging providing a bold contrast to the floor of regular terracotta squares.*

temperatures down inside the house. Slate has the advantage of great depth and variation in colour. It can be grey, green, burgundy or black, and looks as good as stone in any setting, topped perhaps with a kilim or mat in a living room or bedroom.

Many contemporary Mediterranean houses feature 'old stone' floors that have been laid at a fraction of the cost of the real thing. Concrete is coloured to an authentic hue and scored to give the impression of flagstones. Colour is a lively option here, and using shades that are perhaps less than authentic can result in vibrantly toned floors with all the warmth and richness of carpet but still cool to the touch and much less expensive.

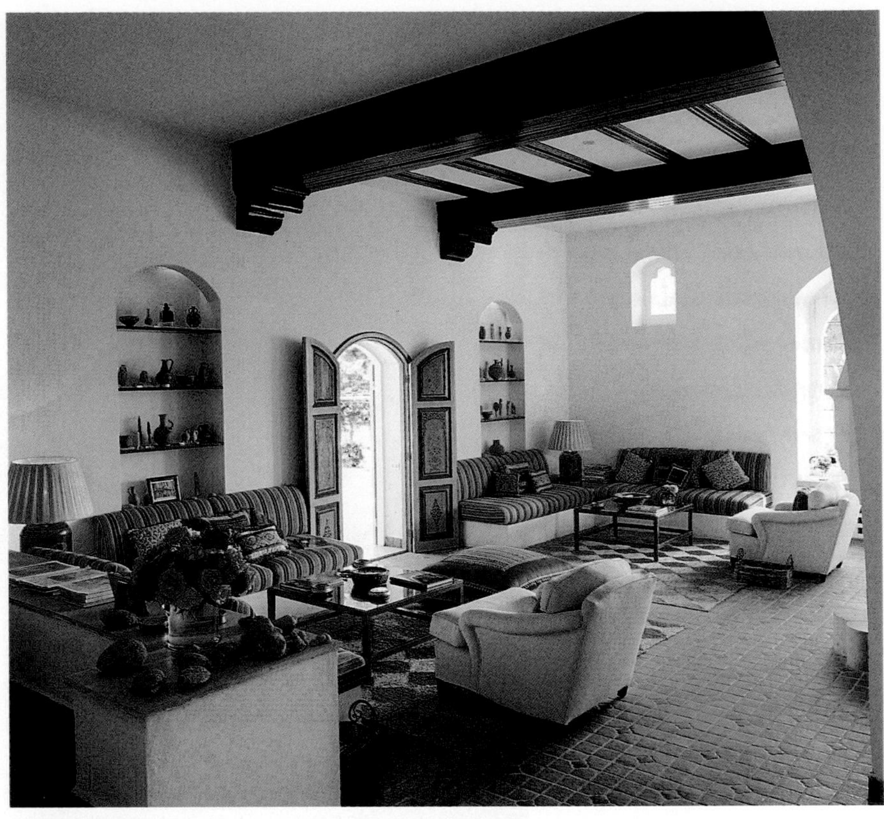

Bricks

Bricks are a versatile form of flooring both inside and outside the house. They can be used on their own or in combination with other materials, such as slate, marble or stone. Traditionally manufactured bricks are quite different from the bright reddish, standardized building blocks used for modern construction; they are smaller, with natural variations in shape, and they are soft in colour, ranging from earthy terracotta to a pale pink. Narrow, darker red bricks are typical of traditional Spanish architecture and are used extensively within the house and leading out into the intricately patterned pathways of the courtyard and garden. In other areas floors are made up of bricks that are almost square in shape. In whatever shape or form, however, they combine to make floors of great character that look warmly inviting and attractive while at the same time being eminently practical and cool.

Above *Enlivened by black lozenge-shaped insets, terracotta paving is a practical option in a sitting room that opens directly on to a garden. The diamond pattern is repeated in the rush mats that define the seating areas.*

Right *Terracotta tiles make an enduring and attractive floor covering for this stylish monochrome bedroom. Although cool in the summer, terracotta is warmer in winter than stone, making it particularly versatile for floors.*

MARBLE

More often associated with the interiors of grand Italian *palazzi*, marble is wonderfully cool. Its satin-smooth finish can be used sparingly to great effect. Hall floors can be lined in marble or marble and slate, while in bathrooms and kitchens it need not be confined to the floor but lends itself to worktops too. Marble tiles are a more accessible alternative to expensive thick slabs of real marble, while terrazzo, a marble-chip composite, makes a colourful and practical variation for more utilitarian areas of the home.

PEBBLES

Many Mediterranean rivers and beaches are a rich source of smooth, round stones. These pebbles, like every abundant local material, have naturally found their way into construction and decoration. Traditionally used en masse, thickly embedded in cement, they are a characteristic sight on many streets and courtyards throughout the region. In Provence, *calade* floors, as they are known, are still being laid today. Traditionally, the pebbles would be thickly set, with little space between the individual stones, creating a cobblestone effect. Being very hard-wearing, and thus perfect for use out of doors, this decorative method has been gradually modified to create a very stylish form of interior flooring.

Inside, the pebbles can be set more sparingly into the cement and fashioned into patterns of surprising delicacy and detail. Lines of pebbles can be used to create borders around the edge of a room or to define an area for

sitting or eating. They can be massed into sections that are arranged at intervals within a floor of conventional stone or tiles. Alternatively they can be set into coloured cement for a more vibrant effect; set high for a very textured look, or low, almost level with the cement, for a smoother feel that would be less disturbing to walk on and easier to keep clean. Surprisingly, pebbles are hugely versatile, giving an artistic imagination the opportunity to run riot.

Pebbles can be found in most countries, but for those people less eager to search for themselves, builders' suppliers are the answer. Glass or wooden beads, shells, or even bits of wood can also be set in this way.

Above *A double line of pebbles gives definition to the plain, polished cement floor of this bathroom. The pebbles are set flush into the cement, with their smoothest side uppermost, to be comfortable to bare feet.*

Facing *Bordered by tiled 'pathways', the floor of this room is inset with pebbles, close-packed like cobblestones. The highly textured effect is softened by the billowing curtains and loosely draped upholstery.*

INSETS

In the same way that border tiles are used to enliven plain walls, so various insets (in different materials and contrasting colours) can be used to add a touch of vitality to an expanse of floor. Replacing a single tile or slab of stone with pebbles is one way of introducing texture and colour, but there are numerous other combinations that are equally typical of Mediterranean interior design.

Small squares or diamonds of colourful patterned ceramic tiles are often inset into plain terracotta tiled floors, perhaps picking up on the colour of the walls or furnishings,

54 ▷

PEBBLED FLOOR

1

2

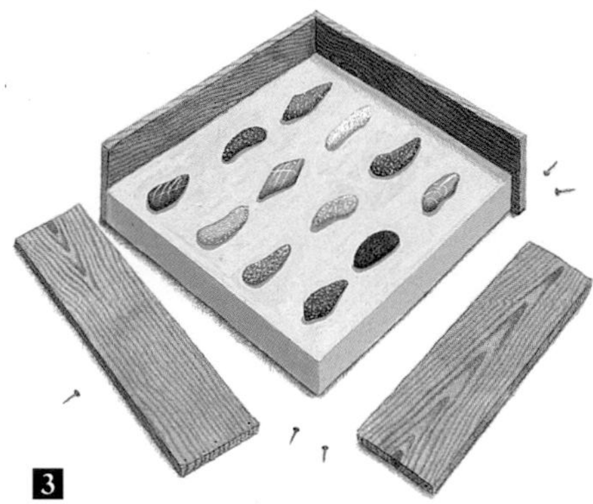
3

TOOLS & MATERIALS

- Large, flat pebbles, washed and dried
- 4 strips of thin wood, plus hardboard
- Hammer and tacks, and spirit level
- Self-levelling compound, polythene (polyethylene), spatula, jug and cloth

METHOD

- Decide on the size of your tiles and construct a mould for them from four pieces of wood. Cut the wood to length, and to a height of at least 5 cm (2 in). Then tack the pieces together to make a frame. Draw a pencil line around the inside to mark the thickness of the tile.
- Place a sheet of polythene (polyethylene) over a piece of flat board and set the mould on top. Check the board and base with a spirit level to make sure that everything is even.
- Mix enough self-levelling compound to make up a third of the total thickness of each tile (four large cups of compound to one of water). Pour the first layer into the mould and leave for about two hours **1**, until it reaches the consistency of putty.
- Mix up and apply a second batch of compound, as before. After leaving this layer for two hours, press the pebbles into it **2**. Smooth out any displaced compound with a spatula.
- Mix a runnier third layer of compound (one-and-a-half large cups of water to four of compound), and pour it up to the pencil line. Use a damp cloth to wipe away any splashes of compound that may have fallen on the pebbles.
- Leave to dry for 24 hours and then release the tile from the mould **3**.

Left *Close-set into concrete, pebbles make a durable and highly textured floor that leads easily out to a pebbled courtyard.*

WINDOWS AND DOORS

WINDOWS AND DOORS

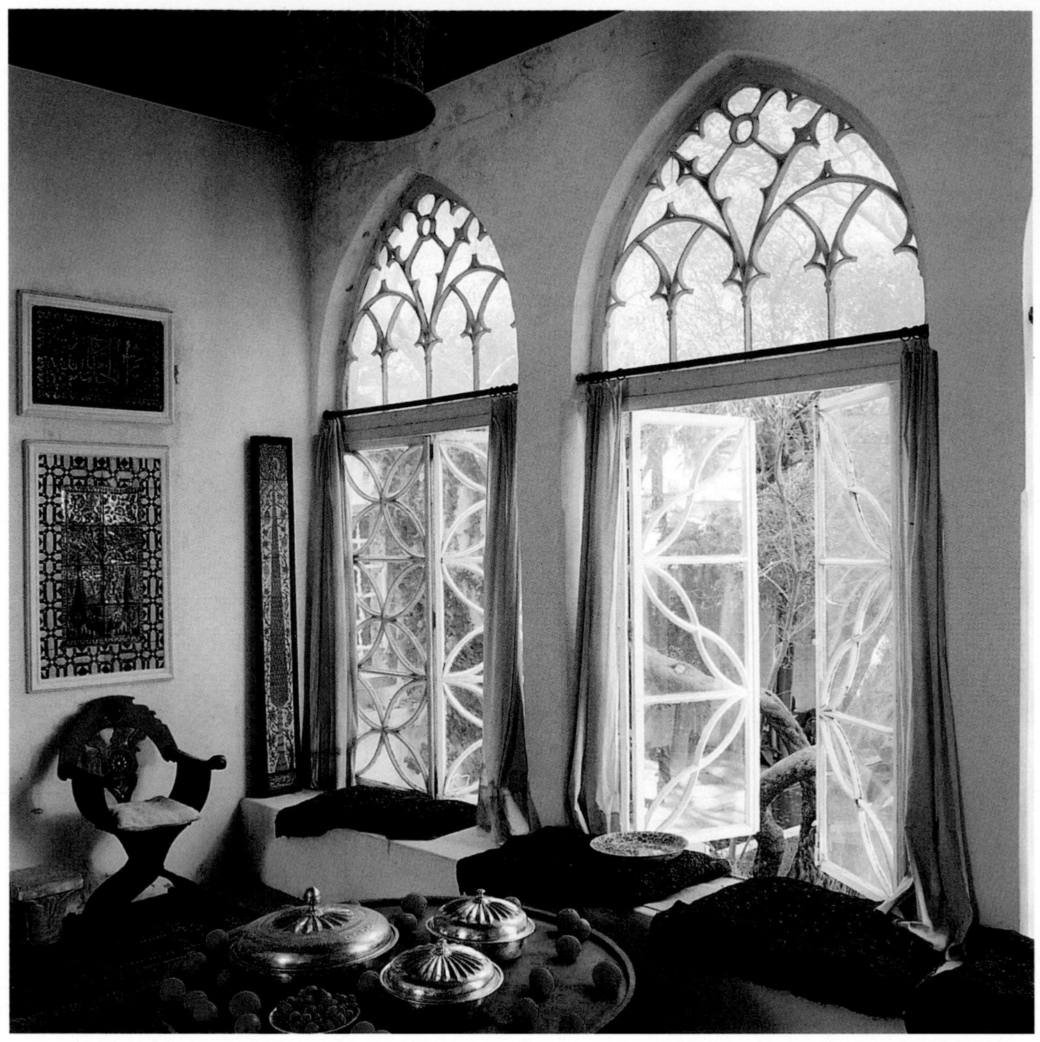

__Above__ Graceful tracery replaces standard glazing bars in these gothic windows, filtering the light as well as strengthening the glass. Bare branches in the garden beyond echo the curvilinear movement.

__Facing__ This gilded, panelled door makes an imposing entrance into a bathroom, holding its own amid the abundant decorative tiling.

Windows and doors of Mediterranean houses are treated less as barriers to the elements than as openings to afford uninhibited access to the rooms inside. It is not often necessary to have them closed to retain heat or keep out the cold or rain. Instead, at times, the heat and light of the sun are so intense that the imperative is to keep the interior cool.

Hence, the windows of Mediterranean houses were traditionally small; large expanses of glazing are much more a feature of cooler climates where the aim is to maximize every minute of sunlight and where there is little danger of over-heating. In old Spanish houses, windows were often placed

high up under the eaves to diffuse the brightness of the light. Grander houses featured windows in the *ajimez* style in which two narrow arches divided by a central column served, successfully, to diffuse the light. In Provence, and elsewhere, farmhouse windows are set deep in thick stone walls.

Where there are larger windows or double doors, they invariably open on to a shady area that prevents the full midday glare from falling directly on the house. In Spain, many large houses had cloistered internal courtyards that afforded the ground floor extra protection from the sun. Sometimes furnished as interior rooms, these provided space to sit and to walk in the heat of the day. Terraces and patios throughout the region are generally shaded by lean-to roofs, canvas awnings, or pergolas covered with creepers such as jasmine and *Dama de la Noche*, which are reputedly repellent to insects – especially mosquitoes.

In an attempt to keep the house as cool as possible, windows and doors are often shaded by shutters and openwork screens, which filter both the light and the heat. Slatted wooden shutters, often brightly painted in vivid contrast to walls, are typically Mediterranean, but ironwork grilles, exterior blinds, awnings and decorative screens are equally characteristic. Kept closed during the day, they soften the light while still allowing cooling breezes to circulate. At night they can be opened to maximize the movement of cool air, or left shut to maintain privacy and security.

Although the open-air lifestyle of the Mediterranean is naturally conducive to a more social way of life – open windows and doors allowing easy communication – privacy is also an important element, particularly in the Islamic countries of the Mediterranean. Hence, the development of fixed screens, as found in the traditional Moroccan *hamman*, and the decorative *reja*, or ironwork grille, that adorns the windows of many historic houses in Spain which, for seven centuries, was under the influence of Islam.

GRILLES

Decorative wrought-iron grilles are typical of many areas of the Mediterranean, especially of Spain where there is a long-standing tradition of metalwork. Although they are fixed permanently in place, they serve a similar function to shutters. They vary in style and design across the region. Some houses feature rather forbidding four-square grilles that are clearly designed to deter intruders, while, by contrast, Spanish *rejas* are highly decorative adornments intended to enhance the façade of the house as well. In fact, the degree of adornment was considered to reflect the wealth and status of the household. In the light behind these elegant and ornate screens, the women could sit and read, or sew, while remaining demurely hidden from passers-by. Just how hidden is a matter of speculation: many a courtship is said to have been initiated at the windows overlooking the street. The *reja* then served as protection not only from marauders but also from the attentions of over-enthusiastic suitors.

In certain cases, the wrought ironwork was combined with glazing to make the window itself decorative, rather in the manner of traditional leaded windows. In these cases, the 'grille' forms a delicate tracery on the glass and filters out the sunlight. This form of window decoration is easily reinvented in a cooler climate, although actively reducing the light coming through a window is perhaps less desirable. To give an unprepossessing window – perhaps with an equally unprepossessing view – a Mediterranean character, use narrow tape or paint in a simple but appropriate design.

WINDOW SCREENS

Open- or fretwork screens originated largely in the Islamic countries of the Mediterranean. They can be found in Moroccan *hammans*, in Turkish harems, in mosques and private houses. They were used both on windows and as internal screens.

Their primary function was to protect the privacy of the women of the household and to divide the worlds of the men and women in public places such as mosques. They also served the same purpose as shutters and grilles, reducing the amount of heat and light entering an interior and thereby keeping the building as cool as possible.

They are delicate in design, using symbolic as well as highly decorative motifs such as the eight-pointed Islamic star. The ceilings of the subterranean baths of the Alhambra palace in Spain are punctured with Islamic stars to give the illusion of night even during the daylight hours. Generally fretwork screens are made of wood, though also occasionally of metal.

Instantly evocative, such a screen could transform a room at a touch. You may not be troubled by an excess of light or heat, but a screen may still be used to camouflage a poor view, perhaps from a window that looks straight on to the back of another building. Equally you could increase the privacy in a bathroom or in a street-side bedroom by erecting a screen in the window. Against stained glass, such screens will create delicate patterns with rainbow-coloured light.

Left *The detailed geometric patterns of the ornamental grilles in these graceful arched windows screen the sun on two sides of the room, leaving the third, more shady side open to the breeze.*

Right *Wrought-iron grilles, fashioned into decorative patterns, are typical of many Spanish houses and were originally designed to provide both shade and security.*

they can be hung anywhere that would benefit from a touch of colour, texture, movement or even wit. In the absence of a suitable doorway they can simply be hung as a colourful and original wall hanging.

Doors

It is easy to forget that at other times and in other cultures doors have frequently had a highly symbolic as well as a practical significance. The door marked the entrance to someone's home and property; not only were enemies dared to cross this threshold, but guests were also welcomed through it. This symbolic language has left a fearsome legacy of drawbridges, moats, portcullises and solid timbered gates and doors, built both to protect occupants and repel invaders. It is also evident in the elaborate doors of churches and mosques that were designed both to welcome and to instruct worshippers by being visually beautiful and telling a richly pictorial story.

Mediterranean doors, too, conform to these same basic criteria. In their simplest form, they are brightly painted to indicate a warm welcome, yet often they can be aggressively studded and adorned with iron hinges and catches to give the impression of immense strength. Larger houses and palaces were built with imposing entrances big enough for a horse and carriage to pass through; their large wooden or iron grille doors often had a smaller door for pedestrians set into them. The grandest examples have survived from the days when elaborately decorated doors were set into a framework of bold architectural detail, such as stone rustication or pillars topped with a broken pediment. The extent of this decoration was an indication of the degree of welcome you might expect from within, and also revealed the lineage, status and power of the occupants. With the rise of powerful families across the region – as, for example, in fifteenth- and sixteenth-century Spain – family escutcheons, or crests, began to be incorporated into the doors of palaces. It was the Church, however, that took

Facing *A wooden door is given great presence by the sturdiness of its construction and the arrangement of twelve panels inscribed with star and cross motifs.*

Right *The ingenious use of trellis has given a characteristic Mediterranean silhouette to these two standard rectangular doorways, creating a feature out of a walk-through dressing room.*

Right below *The lozenge-patterned stained glass in these entrance doors creates a play of light and colour on the black-and-white tiling of the walls and floor.*

STUDDED DOORS

1

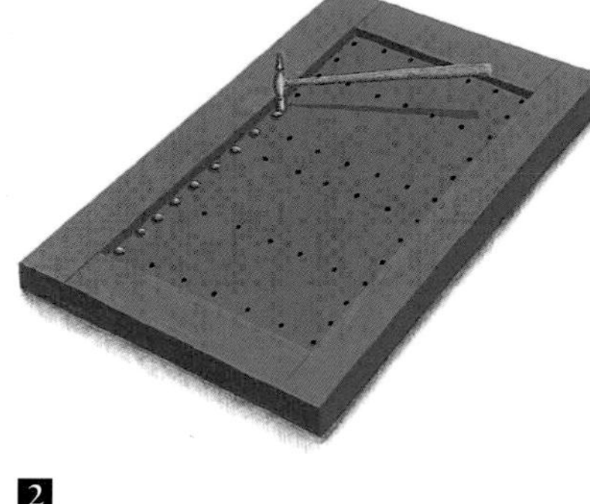

2

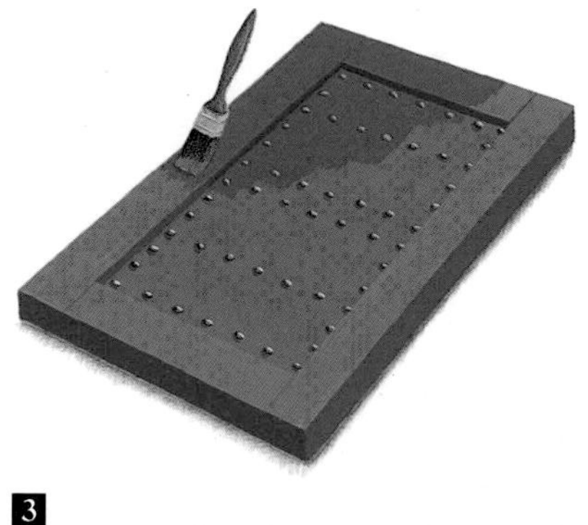

3

TOOLS & MATERIALS

- 2 pieces of chipboard or hardwood
- 8 strips of wood
- Wood adhesive and spreader
- Planer and sandpaper
- Emulsion paint and paintbrush
- Upholstery tacks and hammer
- Screwdriver, screws and drill
- 2 handles and 4 hinges

Studs can be added to existing cabinets, but the doors must be taken down and lain flat before starting work. For new doors, measure your cabinet for the size of the backing boards and the border strips. The tacks should not penetrate through the wood. Decide on the pattern and number of tacks required.

METHOD

- Using a spreader, apply wood adhesive to both backing boards and border strips **1**. Do not 'spot glue'. Allow at least two days for the glue to dry thoroughly.
- Check that the doors fit the cabinet. Leave a gap of approximately 1 mm (1/20 in) between the body of the cabinet and the doors, and between the doors themselves. Plane the doors if necessary and, if using hardwood, lightly rub them with sandpaper before painting.
- Undercoat and paint each door. Start in the centre of the door, and move on to the lower and upper borders, finishing with the sides. Use long strokes for a smooth finish. Allow four hours to dry before marking-up your design with a pencil.
- Hammer the tacks into the doors **2**, and cover with a second coat of paint **3**.
- Once the paint is dry, mark the positions of your handles, drill pilot holes for the screws, and attach the handles to the doors with a screwdriver.
- Attach the hinges, positioning them one-fifth of the way up and down the door. To do this, mark the position of the screws on the door and the cabinet, and drill holes. Attach the hinge one screw at a time, closing the door to check the fit after each screw is in place.

Above *A simple panelled design using black iron studs lends instant character to this flat wooden door, with a wrought-iron handle and knocker to complete the effect.*

Mosaic Tabletop

Tools & Materials

- Simple metal table
- Thick cardboard or plywood
- Tape measure
- Ceramic tiles, tile cutter and pincers
- Carborundum file or sandpaper
- Layout paper and rolling pin
- Wallpaper paste and paintbrush
- Scalpel or scissors
- Waterproof tile adhesive and spreader
- Grout and spatula and sponge
- Round-tipped wooden stick and cloth

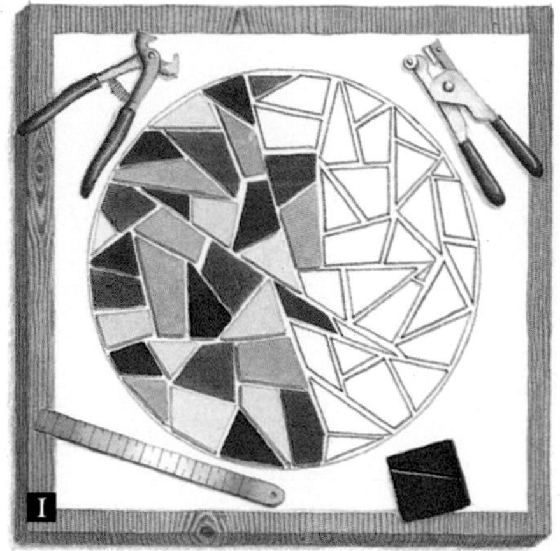

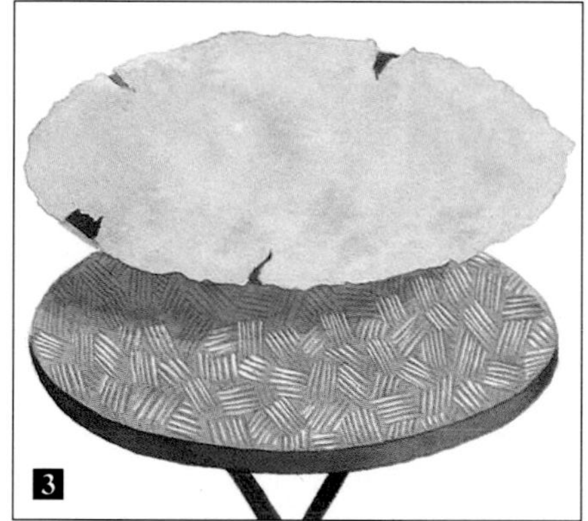

To transfer a design using the paper method, tiles should be no more than 4 mm (1/8 in) thick. Thicker tiles require a simpler design and have to be created in situ. If you have sensitive skin, wear rubber gloves while grouting.

Method

- First measure the tabletop and transfer the dimensions on to a piece of cardboard, remembering to leave space between the mosaic pieces for the grouting.
- Using a tile cutter, score and snap the tiles according to your design. Then lay the tiles on the cardboard, working from the centre outwards **1**. Shapes can be neatened and the table edge defined by scoring and trimming the tiles with the pincers. Smooth any rough edges with a carborundum file or coarse sandpaper. The tile pieces at the edge of the table should be flush, so there is no overhang.

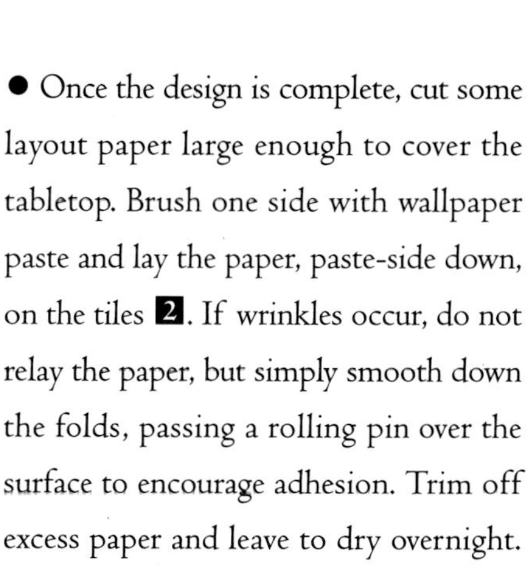

- Once the design is complete, cut some layout paper large enough to cover the tabletop. Brush one side with wallpaper paste and lay the paper, paste-side down, on the tiles **2**. If wrinkles occur, do not relay the paper, but simply smooth down the folds, passing a rolling pin over the surface to encourage adhesion. Trim off excess paper and leave to dry overnight. If any part does not stick, make a small hole in the paper and insert more paste.
- Using the spreader, apply the tile adhesive to the tabletop. With the help of a second person, lift the paper-covered mosaic off the cardboard onto the surface of the table, tile-side down **3**. Check for overhang and adjust if necessary.
- Press the tiles evenly into the adhesive and leave to set for 24 hours. Then dampen the paper with a sponge and remove. Wipe the surface of the tiles clean and trim any tile overhang with pincers.
- Apply the grout between the tiles using a spatula or sponge, filling all crevices with an even covering **4**. Remove excess with a damp cloth and run a round-tipped stick between the tiles for a smooth finish. Leave to dry for 24 hours.

Wall Hanging

Tools & Materials

- Curtain rod – length 1.5 m (59 in), diameter 2 cm (¾ in)
- Base fabric – length 1.5 m (59 in), width 50 cm (20 in), allowing 2 cm (¾ in) extra for hem
- Cardboard
- Extra base fabric for tabs
- Coloured fabric and thread for design
- Scissors, pins, pencil, sewing machine or needle, tape measure, iron
- Tools for hanging curtain rod

Before starting, decide on a suitable curtain rod, the dimensions of the wall hanging, and the fabrics you would like to use. Then plan the design.

1

2

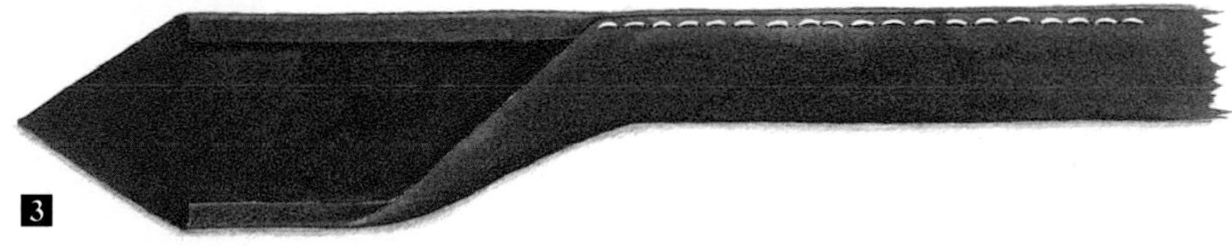

3

Method

- Measure out and cut the backing fabric. The fabric for each of these panels measured 1.5 m (59 in) long and 50 cm (20 in) wide. Leave an extra 2 cm (¾ in) all around for hem, and then pin and hem the border. Cut out cardboard templates according to your design and arrange them on the base fabric **1**.
- Cut out the fabric for each template. Again, leave sufficient turnover for a small hem and then pin the shapes into place on the backing cloth **2**.
- Use the spare backing fabric to make up the tabs. Three tabs were used for each of these panels. (Depending on the length of your curtain rod, you may wish to alter this.) Cut a piece of fabric long enough to loop over the rail and twice the width required. These tabs are 12 cm [4¾ in] long and 12 cm [4¾ in] wide before folding and 6 cm [2⅜ in] wide after folding. Add 1 cm (⅜ in) all around for the hem.

Press and cut the corners of the tab at a diagonal before folding and pressing the width-ends down to the wrong side. Then fold or iron the fabric in half, lengthways, and stitch all the sides 3 mm (⅛ in) from the edge **3**.

- Machine sew all the pieces into place. Alternatively, hand sew the shapes using a small stitch. Remember to change the colour of the thread according to the colour of each piece of fabric.

Sew the tabs on to the hanging at 16 cm (6⅜ in) intervals. The number of tabs and the length between them will depend on the width of your fabric. Once the tabs are in place, iron the final piece.

Attach the curtain rod to the wall, and finally slide the loops over the rail to hang the finished panel.

Corona and Canopy

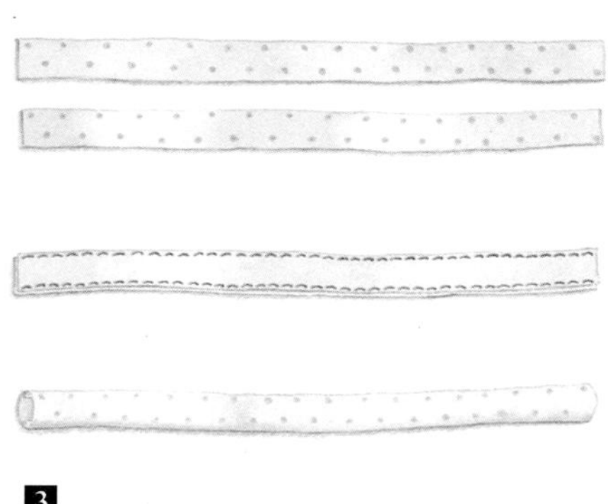

Tools & Materials

- Corona kit or flexible curtain track
- Sheer cotton fabric
- Tape measure
- Sewing scissors
- Sewing machine and iron
- Pins, needle and thread
- Curtain rings (if making your own corona)

Corona kits can sometimes be purchased, or alternatively, you can make a corona by attaching flexible curtain track to a wooden batten and fixing this to the ceiling. The canopy fabric should be sheer and lightweight – we used voile. The number of sections will depend on the bed size and the height of the corona; this canopy was made in six sections.

Method

- For a mosquito-proof canopy, stitch the sections together and drape a short length of fabric over the top.
- Measure the circumference of the corona and divide this by the number of sections required to give the width of each section. For the fabric length, measure down to the floor from the position of the corona above the bed.
- Mark on the fabric the width of the top edge of the first canopy section, centering this on the fabric edge. Mark the length to which the fabric is to be cut, tapering out from the top **1**. Then cut out each of the sections in this way.
- Hem all sides of each section by making two folds of 6 mm (¼ in) each, pressing and pinning along the length of the fold. Machine stitch to make a neat double hem.
- Join the sections of fabric at the top by slip stitching the side edges together for a distance of about 15 cm (6 in) **2**. Then stitch the curtain rings to the top corners of each section.
- Make ties to attach to the curtain rings by cutting two fabric strips to the length and width of your choice – ours were 40 x 4 cm (16 x 1½ in). Machine stitch the strips together along the long edges and then turn them right-side out **3**. Cover the corona hoop and the chains attaching the corona to the ceiling in the same way, but cut the chain strips long enough to ruffle the fabric.

Left *A sheer muslin corona softens the effect of rough-hewn walls and a pebbled floor.*

Hot-house cut flowers rarely feature in the Mediterranean house, and a bunch of wild flowers in a simple jug is far more typical. Cut flowers are displayed in loose, informal arrangements. Seasonal blooms are mixed with plenty of foliage and are displayed in containers that are often simple and functional, but beautiful in themselves. However, arrangements of dried flowers, grasses and twigs are longer-lasting, and although they lack the vibrant colour of fresh flowers, they can produce a dramatically sculptural effect, which is intensified if set against a simple decorative scheme – a plain rough-plastered wall, or a broad expanse of paint. The more pronounced seasons can be awkward in non-Mediterranean climates but bought flowers can add a colourful note all year round and alternatives might include pots of lilies or orchids that can be nurtured to bloom in winter.

Large terracotta water or olive-oil jars, flowerpots of all shapes and sizes, tubs, urns, baskets and blue-and-white ceramic pots all make striking containers. Ordinary terracotta flowerpots are versatile and cheap. They can be 'aged' or 'distressed' for added authenticity by painting them with a grey- or brown-tinted wash, or they can be painted in bold, bright colours for a sunnier effect. Grouping small pots together rather than dotting them about in isolation has greater visual impact.

Employing garden implements decoratively in a room underlines the notion of bringing the outside – with all its textures and materials – indoors. Antique garden tools are especially highly prized and can look striking hung on the wall, while flower baskets, flowerpots and watering cans can be displayed on shelves or pegs. Hats are also wonderfully

Right *Bringing the outside inside: flowers, fruit and foliage fill almost every available surface in this dining room, displayed in a variety of containers – baskets of wire and wicker, pots and mosaic vases.*

evocative and a row of wide-brimmed straw hats randomly hung on the wall will immediately conjure up a picture of long, lazy summer days. Nothing is more dampening to a warm, sunny ambience than rows of heavy winter coats, which are best concealed in closets.

Baskets

Baskets feature throughout the Mediterranean region in a wide range of natural materials; they are usually handmade, their sizes and shapes bearing witness to their myriad traditional functions. Inherently beautiful, they can be displayed on walls or shelves; they can also be used to display other items, such as fruit and vegetables; or they can become functional containers – for firewood, magazines, newspapers or sewing materials. Look again at your kitchen: bread, cheese, and crackers look far more appealing served in shallow open baskets rather than on ordinary plates, while deeper, more rigid baskets make excellent containers for root vegetables, dry foods such as cereals and pasta, or even items for recycling. Even a large, round basket that might originally have been strapped across the back of a donkey carrying produce to market can be put to good use as a laundry basket.

Wood

Like basketry, wood usually combines form and function, the decorative and the practical. Unpainted and unadorned with carving or inlay, the natural grain and colour of wood looks beautiful, whether as receptacle or ornament. Wood sits easily throughout the home, in harmony with the heavier structural timbers, or against the background of a wooden floor. Incorporating one or two small wooden pieces in a plainly furnished room will emphasize the simplicity that is so characteristic of Mediterranean style. A smooth bowl in olive wood will just ask to be touched, and the smell and feel of it will conjure up images of hazy olive groves; turned

candlesticks, rustic frames, wooden trays and platters will lend force to the illusion. Specific examples of indigenous wood craftsmanship – carvings or sculptures, inlaid furniture or boxes – will refer anyone directly to the countries from which they have been brought.

Pebbles and stones

Potent images of the Mediterranean can be evoked using relatively humble objects, such as a collection of smooth, round stones from a local river bed. Alternatively, jagged pieces of semi-precious stones will catch the light and sparkle brightly. In some areas there is an abundance of marble too, veined in glowing iridescent colours and polished into smooth shapes that are satisfyingly heavy and tactile.

Shells

It is the sea and seashore that evoke most magically the essence of the Mediterranean. Objects collected from the beach or under the water, ranging from a twisted, gnarled piece of driftwood, bleached by sea and the sun, to honey-coloured natural sponges, starfish and shells, can be displayed either individually or as collections – not just in the watery domain of the bathroom, but anywhere in the house. Even sand of varying colours and degrees of fineness can be poured into tall glass jars and corked to maintain the moisture level within and thereby the original colours. The biggest shells are best displayed as single objects, while smaller ones can be used for more ornamental projects – glue them on to mirror frames, or to the lids of wooden boxes or lamp bases.

Left *Pink oleander flowers and fresh figs are placed alongside a stone sink, providing flashes of brilliant colour. The terracotta jug and glazed earthenware containers are both practical and decorative.*

STORAGE

Storage throughout the Mediterranean home is uncontrived and unpretentious, and cupboard space is not concealed or disguised. Its function is paramount and its decorative value appears incidental – certainly not planned.

Shelving is an essential element in Mediterranean storage, and although books and ornaments may sometimes be displayed behind glass, they will more often live on open wooden shelves. Some shelving will be constructed as the house itself is built, in alcoves either side of the fireplace, above doors, or in the kitchen – plastered and painted with the walls. More informal shelves, constructed as the need demands, will scramble across the wall. Usually made of wood, they may be left untreated, to echo the exposed beams or floorboards in the room, or may be colourfully painted.

It is in the Mediterranean kitchen that storage plays its most important role. Here, simplicity and informality are underpinned by a love of good food and fine cooking. The Mediterranean kitchen may look simple, even a little rustic, but as witnessed by the standard of cuisine, it is in fact surprisingly well planned. Free standing cupboards of varying heights and designs contain much of the cooking paraphernalia. They need not match each other, nor anything else in the room, but all of them have a function and are therefore essential to the overall look.

Kitchen shelves often appear to have been carved out of the wall – indeed, in some traditional farmhouses where the walls are thick enough, they may well have been. Alternatively, they may be constructed to look like niches – sometimes arched to echo the architecture of the region. They are often

Left *A range of whitewashed open shelves provides easily accessible storage for china in everyday use. Homemade preserves are left to mature on the top.*

Above facing *Propped-up on a high shelf running over the doorway, a selection of ceramic plates and bowls adds colour and decorative relief to plain, white kitchen walls.*

Below facing *Even the modern microwave has its niche in this carefully designed set of shelves, which exploits every inch of the restricted space. Decorative items, however, such as bowls, plates and glasses, take centre stage.*

quirkily crooked, and they are invariably open, ensuring that items are easily reached and turning the often decorative features of kitchen equipment to best advantage.

However, practicality is as important as decoration. The row of bright painted plates displayed along the top shelf will be used for Sunday lunch. Glass storage jars may be aesthetically pleasing but they provide instant access to various ingredients – pasta, herbs and spices – making them ideal for a cook working quickly. Kitchen implements hang on hooks avoiding the need to rummage in a drawer every time they are required. Pots and pans line up alongside pottery and glassware, but the overall effect is still ornamental.

Although a truly Mediterranean kitchen may be out of reach, there are ways in which something of the same atmosphere can be evoked. Painting fitted units in bold, bright colours, or laying terracotta tiles on the floor, makes a strong statement. Decorate cupboard doors using the studding technique (shown on pages 80-81), or apply stencilled or cut-out motifs to minimize uniformity. If possible, use both fitted

Painted Tea Glasses

1

2

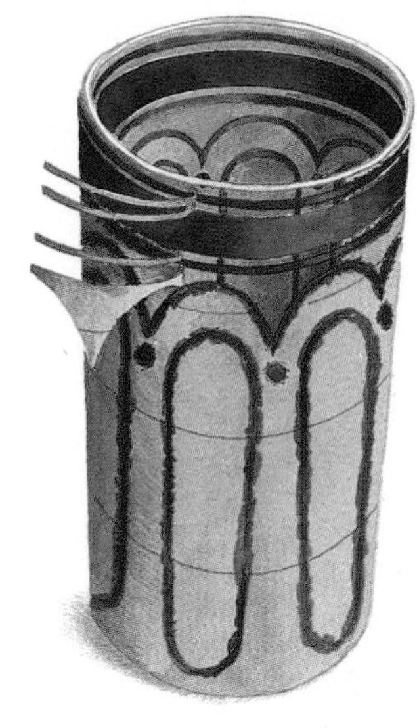

3

Tools & Materials

- Tea or drinking glasses
- Masking tape, scalpel or craft knife
- Artist's round and flat brush
- Glass paint (2 colours, including gold or silver). Use non-toxic glass paint, or avoid painting near the rim of the glass.

Method

- Choose 4–6 plain drinking glasses. Then work out your design on paper – we used a simple linear design, but you might prefer to create a more intricate pattern with loops or scallops.
- When choosing a colour scheme, use gold or silver to outline the design and add detail with strong primary colours. To paint the glasses, you will need a round watercolour brush and special glass paint, available from artists' suppliers and some craft shops. Some glass paints are self-drying; others require the painted glass to be baked in an oven to fix the colour on to the glass. The latter technique is recommended, since it tends to be more colourfast and is more likely to withstand repeated washing.
- First wash the glass and polish it thoroughly with a towel. Then cover the glass completely with masking tape. Cut out paper templates as required and transfer your design on to the glass in pencil 1. Save the templates to use when decorating the other glasses.
- Use a scalpel or craft knife to cut out and remove those areas of the masking tape where paint is to be applied 2.
- Working with an artist's brush, begin to apply the gold or silver paint to the exposed glass. To avoid smudging the paint, place the glass over one hand and turn the base as you work. Use long, lengthwise brushstrokes to give a smooth finish; you may find it easier to use a slightly broader, flat brush to avoid streaks when painting larger areas of glass. Clean your brush in water before applying the second colour.
- Complete the pattern by filling in the areas of the glass still exposed, using the second colour. Remove all remaining masking tape 3. Check the pattern and tidy up uneven lines by scraping off excess paint with your scalpel.
- Repeat the process to decorate the other glasses. Bake all the glasses gently in the oven to seal the paint. The baking time will vary according to the manufacturer's instructions, but will probably be around 20 minutes.
- Remove the glasses from the oven and allow them to cool.

LIGHTING

Just as natural materials predominate in the Mediterranean home, so natural light is exploited to the full. In the summer it is more often a case of trying to soften the intensity of the sunlight, in order to minimize any harsh effects on the furnishings. Filtering out the sunlight also helps to maintain an even, cool temperature inside the house. However, on darker days and in the evenings any natural light will need to be augmented. In keeping with the emphasis on nature and natural materials that underpins Mediterranean decorating, artificial light tends to be subtle and diffuse, replicating the warm tones and deep contrasts of the naturally lit interior.

CANDLELIGHT

Candlelight is the most effective way of introducing additional light in the Mediterranean home. Its gentle, flickering glow enhances any setting and is instantly evocative of warm, velvety evenings. Most often placed on the dining table, candles can also be used in wrought-iron chandeliers, or in wall sconces, and they can be arrayed in candlesticks and other less conventional holders of varying size on mantelpieces and tables. Georgian silver or fine porcelain candlesticks would probably look out of place; those made with natural materials such as plain wood, clay, pottery and wrought iron are more appropriate set against a simple rough-plastered, colourwashed wall. Alternatively, try floating night lights in water in a simple glass or pottery bowl; or stand candles in small terracotta flowerpots, wedging them in oasis (florist's foam) and covering the candle base with bright green moss. Use plain cream or golden beeswax candles for a truly natural effect.

Candlelit chandeliers should not be suspended so high that they are out of reach: a position directly above the dining table would be more suitable than over a stairwell. Characteristically made in slender black wrought ironwork,

they look best with cream candles and, to avoid drips of wax, should have generous holders. Wall sconces might also be of wrought iron, though brass, wood and pottery are possible alternatives. In a Mediterranean house a single sconce might be the only feature on an otherwise completely plain wall; symmetry and neat pairing seems of little importance in this very informal style of decoration.

Candle lanterns, which protect the flame from breezes, make it possible to eat out-of-doors as dusk draws in. They can be used as permanent fixtures indoors, too; they range from elegantly curved glass storm lanterns, designed specifically to stand on tabletops, through hanging lanterns that can be suspended from beams or hooks. If necessary, it is possible to vary their height by hanging them from a length of chain. In finishes such as brass, black metal or verdigris, lanterns are particularly useful for areas such as hallways where overhead lighting may be necessary.

Oil storm lamps and lanterns are similarly atmospheric. The light they offer is soft and mellow, although it should be more constant than candlelight if the wick is at the correct height. Resilient in even quite strong gusts, they are particularly useful for illuminating al fresco suppers; their light is stronger than candlelight, and more predictable. Storm lamps are often decoratively curvaceous, making them very adaptable for use inside the house. Cleverly positioned, they may emphasize the shape of an arched alcove or doorway, or a round table. So sympathetic are these lamps and lanterns that electrified versions are now much more readily available than original ones.

Left *Candlelight from a row of tiny night lights in glass holders provides an ambient glow, which is reflected in the glazed urns below. A pierced metal ceiling-hung lantern provides the option for a more general light.*

Right *A striking combination of natural and artificial lighting: sunlight streams through the window, while wall lights are concealed behind decoratively cut plaster holders-cum-shades, and candlelight illuminates the arched wall niches.*

Facing *This ornamental lantern, in glass and metal, suspended from a simply painted beamed ceiling, is just one example of the myriad styles of lantern found around the Mediterranean; fixed or portable, they are traditionally powered by candles or oil.*

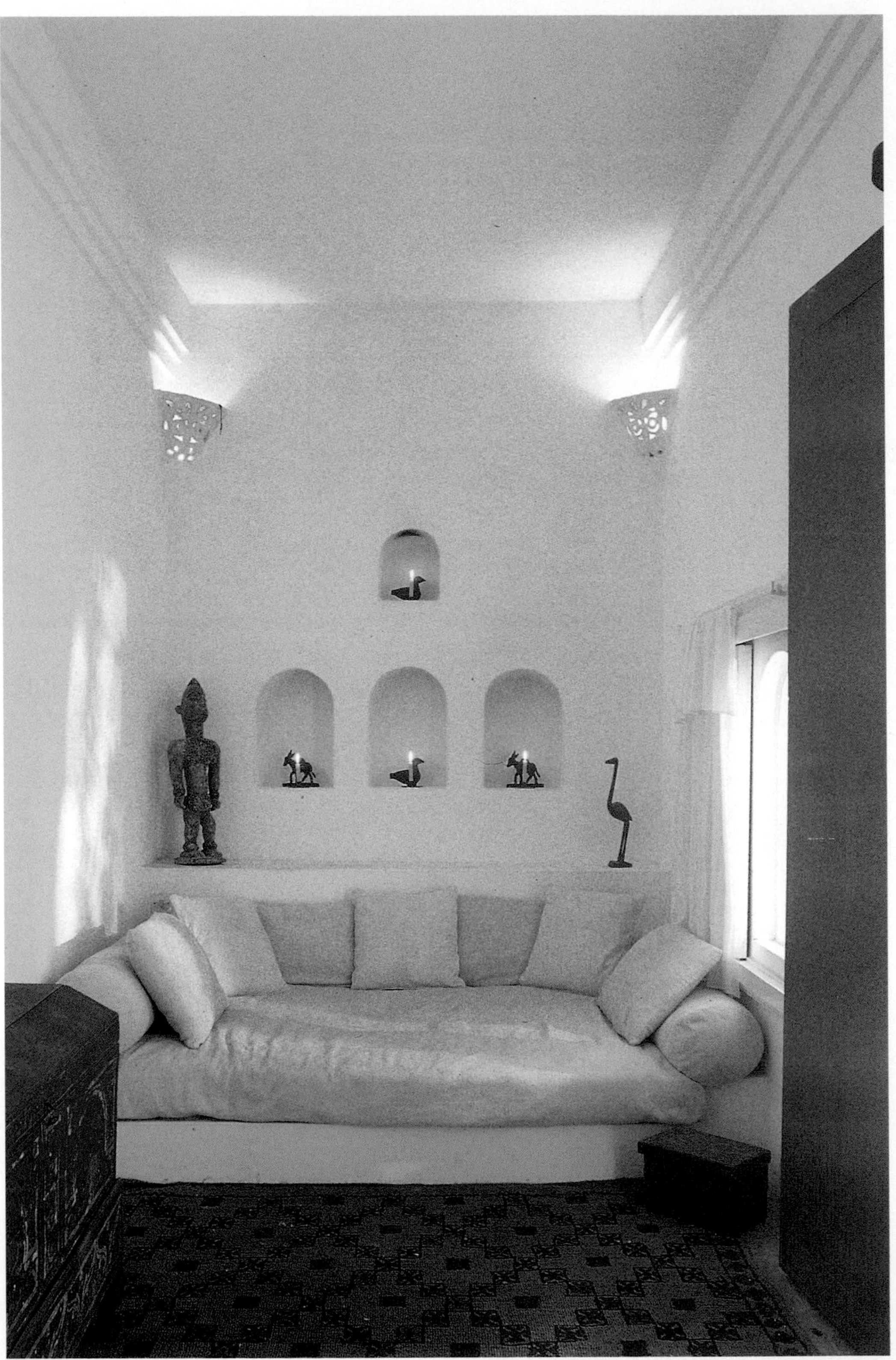

ARTIFICIAL LIGHT

When artificial light is called in to play it must be kept soft and diffused throughout the house. The emphasis is on table, floor and wall lamps rather than overhead lighting, which may introduce unwanted glare. The best and most atmospheric effects are created by combining light from a variety of well-chosen sources. Include candle-light, if possible, for mood and effect, and then add electrified light from one or more wall sconces for general illumination, together with a table lamp and perhaps one large floor lamp. The lamps and lights themselves should not to be a uniform shape and size; a better option is an eclectic collection of individual pieces. Lamp bases are typically made of natural materials such as turned wood, pottery or stone.

Candle bulbs can be substituted for candles in the wall-bracket sconces, as well as in chandeliers. Sconces can be made to appear almost integral to the wall, with the bulb set into a semi-circular bowl that casts a soft light upwards rather than outwards. Although sometimes left plain, the bowl is often pierced with small decorative holes to create intricate patterns of light. Painting the bowl in the same tone as the walls renders it almost invisible, so that the final effect blends well with the decorative scheme.

Lamps that stand on the floor should be large and imposing, otherwise they may look insignificant. A single large church candlestick that was once highly gilded but is now evocatively distressed would be suitably bold. An antique urn or a curvaceous terracotta pot originally used to hold olive oil or carry water would be equally effective. If space is at a premium, the same level of illumination may be achieved by concealing a small uplighter behind a plant or a piece of furniture, although the visual impact of the floor lamp will be lost.

Large, curvy table lamp bases in naturally textured ceramic or painted wood, distressed down to an appropriately aged patina, look good topped with generous lamp shades in parchment tones, whatever the decorative scheme of the room. New lamp bases can be 'aged' very simply, using sandpaper and/or a coloured wash. Similarly, a wash of colour or even well-steeped tea can give a new cream shade instant antiquity. Punching decorative motifs out of the shade, perhaps around the top and base or even across the whole shade, creates an interesting pattern of light on the wall behind.

Modern-looking lights have no place here.but the huge range of modern lighting techniques can be enormously helpful in creating the warm, atmospheric glow of the Mediterranean in a non-Mediterranean climate. Concealed uplighters will cast a wash of light on to a wall and, if appropriate, they may be used to illuminate a particularly striking object or wall hanging. Recessed spotlights, set into the ceiling, will create pools of 'sunlight', and will help to brighten up dark areas such as passageways and corners. Similarly, 'soft-tone' or coloured bulbs will create a warm, diffused glow and are widely available from most hardware shops. Finally, the installation of dimmer switches is a simple and highly effective option, giving you total flexibility and allowing for an instant change of atmosphere at the touch of a button.

Outdoor Living

The outdoor 'rooms' of a Mediterranean house are almost as important a part of the living space as the interior. Larger houses are traditionally built around a courtyard or patio, a direct descendant of the Roman atrium, which formed an enclosed area that was at once both sheltered and shady. Alternatively, a converted farm dwelling or smaller village house might be extended with a paved terrace, oriented to the west in order to benefit from the evening light, and sheltered by retaining walls or creeper-covered trellis.

Two factors are important in the design and development of these outdoor spaces. The first is the summer heat which can be intense. Houses are therefore designed to be kept as cool as possible; hence, the overhanging roofs around a cloistered courtyard, or the leafy shade of a well-planted pergola. Both deflect the intensity of the sun's rays and provide a relatively cool outdoor room that benefits from any passing breeze. The second factor is the wind which, in certain seasons, is a blight on the otherwise balmy Mediterranean climate. More accurately, there are several ferocious and intrusive winds – the French mistral, the Spanish tramontana, the Italian bora and the hot dry sirocco of northern Africa. They occur at different times of the year, but all necessitate effective shelter, especially where the style of architecture is geared towards outdoor living. The enclosed courtyard again provides a perfect solution, giving both shade and shelter.

The high surroundings walls typical of such courtyards cast long shadows which retain as much moisture as possible in the ground in summer. Since the courtyard is surrounded by the house itself, doors and windows looking on to it can be left wide open in hot weather without fear of intrusion and with no loss of privacy. The courtyard also protects the house against any battering from high winds, effectively guarding the windows and doors from driven dust or debris.

Above *In this tranquil corner, shelter from the sun and wind is provided by a wall, with a flight of steps built right into the hillside. A curtain of trailing greenery increases the sense of enclosure.*

Left *Shaded by a cane lean-to roof, an open terrace becomes a comfortable place to sit, even in the heat of the day. The beamed construction blends well with the rough-rendered stone façade of the house.*

WALLS AND WOODWORK

Decorative finishes for patios, terraces and garden rooms often take their cue from the design of the adjacent house: stone follows stone, brick builds on brick, paint on paint, render on render. A typical garden room in Provence, for example, might be surrounded by walls of rough stone and mortar, either whitewashed or left untreated, or they might just as easily have been rendered in characteristic pinky-red, offset by smoky-blue shutters and doors. The historic patios of Cordoba in Spain, on the other hand, are limewashed annually, often with a broad band of coloured wash in light Moroccan blue to soften the glare.

The durability of any paint used is an important issue – it helps to be aware of how it will fare over time. Not only will it have to withstand the force of the weather, but it will also become increasingly difficult to maintain without causing damage to plants as they become established. Natural brick and stone are good choices as they need little attention; alternatively, coloured renders, which age gently as the years pass, give a more consciously decorative impression.

Do not underestimate the effects of colour in an outdoor room. It can be just as evocative outside as in – perhaps more so when juxtaposed against white. A coat of brilliant white paint offset by electric blue or vivid turquoise, for example, immediately conjures up the atmosphere of a seaside village. Softer reds, golds and terracottas, on the other hand, look inland to the warm tones of Provence, the earthy north African palette and the glowing colours of Italian frescoes. The choice will be dictated, in part, by the design of the house, but the amount of space available should also be considered: a small, enclosed patio might need simple white walls to open out the space visually, whereas a larger, more extensive garden room might lend itself to the warm earthy colours that would create an appropriate backdrop for a curtain of evergreen planting.

Doors and woodwork, window frames and shutters, ceiling beams and pergola supports are all potential canvases for the effective use of paint. Striking contrasts of colour and texture are typical of the Mediterranean, with broad bands of colour outlining doors and windows, or simply breaking up plain expanses of wall. Shutters, doors and window frames are almost always painted in a different shade to the house itself, creating a bold counterpoint. Using colour contrasts in this way can be a highly effective and relatively easy way to create a Mediterranean look in cooler, more subdued surroundings.

Above *Artistic illusion: the saffron walls of this enclosed patio have been 'opened up' by a series of trompe l'oeil arches, revealing the prospect of a shimmering blue sea and sky beyond.*

Facing *An exterior wall, plastered in a natural tone, is given a colourful focal point in the shape of an arched doorway, painted in a harlequin pattern; a more affordable version of a highly ornate, heavy wooden door.*

Distempered Wall

Tools & Materials

- 10 kg (20 lb) whiting
- 6 cups rabbit-skin glue powder or PVA (polyvinyl acrylic)
- Stiff brush, bleach, sand and cement
- Small tin of artist's powder paint (try terracotta or other warm colours such as yellow ochre)
- 4–5 tablespoons glycerine
- Bucket
- Paintbrush and newspaper
- Small pan for heating glue
- Large saucepan
- Stick for stirring glue/distemper

Make only as much distemper as you will need for a day's work, since the mixture dries out quickly.

Method

- Remove any dirt from the walls with a stiff brush and treat areas of mould by applying a solution of bleach. Rinse thoroughly with water and allow to dry. Then fill any holes or cracks with a mixture of sand and cement before applying a base coat of emulsion. Allow about five hours for the emulsion to dry thoroughly.
- Half-fill a bucket with cold water and pour in the whiting until it forms a peak above the surface of the water. Leave overnight until the mixture has settled, then pour off the top 5 cm (2 in) of clear water and stir to form a smooth paste.

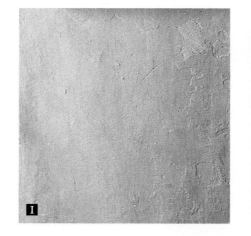

- Prepare the glue according to the manufacturer's instructions. Coarse rabbit-skin granules will need to be soaked overnight in cold water. You will need 6 cups of rabbit-skin glue powder to 6 litres (10 pints) of water, or 6 cups of PVA to 6 cups of water.
- Dissolve the powder paint in a little water and add to the whiting paste a spoonful at a time until you achieve the desired shade. Then mix thoroughly.
- Transfer the prepared glue to a container and place this in a large pan of hot water, taking care that the water does not come over the sides. Heat gently, stirring from time to time, until the glue is runny.
- Pour the warm glue into the coloured whiting paste to make the distemper (one-part glue to nine-parts paste). Stir thoroughly.
- Add one tablespoon of glycerine per litre (2 pints) of distemper. This will prevent the distemper from drying out too quickly when it is applied to the wall.

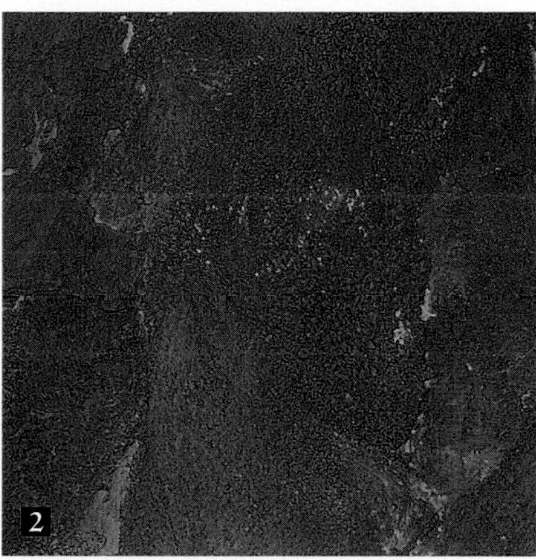

The first coat of distemper should be the consistency of standard emulsion paint.

- Working quickly, apply the first coat, making broad, loose brushstrokes in all directions. Leave some areas of the base coat uncovered. Allow at least 24 hours for it to dry before applying the second coat.
- For the second wash, thin the distemper with water until it is the consistency of milk. Cover the ground with newspaper and apply the wash as quickly as possible. Work over the distemper repeatedly to prevent it from running. Leave only a few areas of white base coat still uncovered, and allow to dry for 24 hours.
- Apply a third coat in the same way, completely covering the base coat.

Above *Chalky paint finishes suit the spectrum of Mediterranean colours from the softest of sea greens* **1** *to the sunniest of oranges* **2**.

Outdoor Relaxing

Left *The soft grey patina of metal, wood and clay is the unifying theme of this airy verandah. Lengths of sun-bleached fabric billow in the breeze, providing shade and an unrestricted view.*

Right *The symmetrical arrangement of furniture and the draped fabric of deck chairs, sun canopy and curtain recall the cool formality of a Roman atrium.*

Comfort and shade

Effective shade is vital when creating a comfortable outdoor room, as it ensures that this space can be used throughout the day – even at the height of a Mediterranean summer. Architectural features that provide a solution to this problem are common throughout the region, and styles range from Spanish cloisters, with their intricately carved ceilings, to the simple, arched verandahs of Italy. Equally efficient, although structurally less solid, are lean-to roofs made from natural fibres like bamboo, or frameworks of wood or metal draped in canvas cloth. These, along with overhanging plants, offer protection by filtering the sunlight in ever-changing patterns of light and shade, while also allowing whatever lazy breeze there might be to penetrate. Finally, big plantation-style umbrellas, which can be moved around as the day progresses, offer a more flexible alternative.

A solid structure will offer a retreat from the sun, as well as providing effective shelter from less-than-perfect weather. For roofing materials, natural fibres are an attractive option and will give good shade, although they may need to be renewed quite frequently. Canvas, on the other hand, may not necessarily provide full protection from the sun.

Outdoor areas close to the house lend themselves to a lean-to arrangement. Use materials that harmonize with the main structure, as these will give the best results. Pergolas can also be effective and may be attached to the house or remain free standing. A simple pergola may consist of strong cross-beams projecting from the house wall and supported at the other end by sturdy wooden uprights or brick pillars. Even quick-growing plants with abundant foliage might not produce the required amount of shade in the first year, but a planted area can evolve gradually, more plants being added each year

to increase the density of shade if necessary. By combining a number of fragrant climbing plants the area will not only look but smell wonderful too. Grape vines and jasmine are typically Mediterranean but need to be planted in a fairly sheltered spot to do best in the more severe conditions in non-Mediterranean climates. Honeysuckle and climbing roses thrive outdoors even in cooler climates. They complement one another perfectly and, grown together, will quickly form a dense canopy of foliage and flowers.

No room, indoors or out, is complete without furniture. The Mediterranean garden room is in use almost all year round and consequently the furniture tends to be as comfortable and well designed as any inside the house. However, outdoor furniture must also be weather-resistant and mobile. Outdoor chairs are typically made of wood or wrought iron, often topped with cushions that can be removed for easy cleaning or if the weather changes. They are either left natural or painted, and although paint may bleach in the sun, the faded distressed effect can be just as attractive as the original hue. Deep-cushioned wicker armchairs and chaises longues in teak or curvy wrought iron combine elegance with comfort. Folding garden seats with painted wooden slats on a metal frame are light and versatile and can be matched with small occasional tables. To introduce a touch of informality, use canvas deck chairs in bold, bright colours.

The ultimate in moveable furniture is perhaps the hammock, strung between two trees or suspended from roof beams. They are most comfortable if made of cool cotton rather than scratchy rope, and the more decorative types are finished with a tasselled fringe. A pillow and a good book are all that is necessary to create the perfect place to rest in the heat of the day.

Left *Blue and green mosaic tiles lend depth to a courtyard pool with its ornamental central basin. The containers and their plantings echo the colour scheme.*

Facing *Water was one of the most prized elements of early Islamic gardens and the rose one of the most favoured plants. Here the two combine, with the petals making a brief splash of colour on the surface of a marble basin.*

FOCUS ON WATER

When the Moors invaded Spain in the eighth century they brought with them a strongly held Islamic belief in the garden as an earthly paradise. The principles governing gardens and the symbolism behind them were, in essence, laid down in the writings of the Koran. Designed with the same rhythm and geometry that characterize the pattern of an oriental carpet, the garden was intended as a peaceful retreat from the outside world, soothing the senses with the gentle sound of water and the fragrance of flowers.

Water and shade were the two most prized elements of the Moorish garden, much valued by a people who originated from desert lands. This love of water reached its zenith in the gardens of the Alhambra, which remain the most ingenious and extraordinary feat of Moorish aquatic engineering. Almost every Spanish courtyard, patio and garden has a fountain or pool, ranging from simple granite basins to more elaborate pools decorated with ornate sculptures. Almudaina in Palma de Mallorca, originally built for King James II, even featured a garden bathroom, complete with hot and cold running water.

The important role of water in landscape design stretches right across the Mediterranean – from the monumental gardens of the Italian Renaissance that feature magnificent cascades and formal fountains, to the shallow pools – sometimes ceramic-lined, sometimes lily-filled – that grace many domestic gardens. Even a small fountain delights the senses with the continuous sound of flowing water, while a still, dark pool can lend hidden depth to a simple courtyard planting of evergreen-lined paths.

No planting scheme will survive a long, hot summer without regular watering. Sprinkler systems and a network of pipes considerably reduce the daily chore of watering but should be installed before planting takes place. Pools and other water features may also require skimmer systems and filters, which will help to keep the water clear in hot conditions.

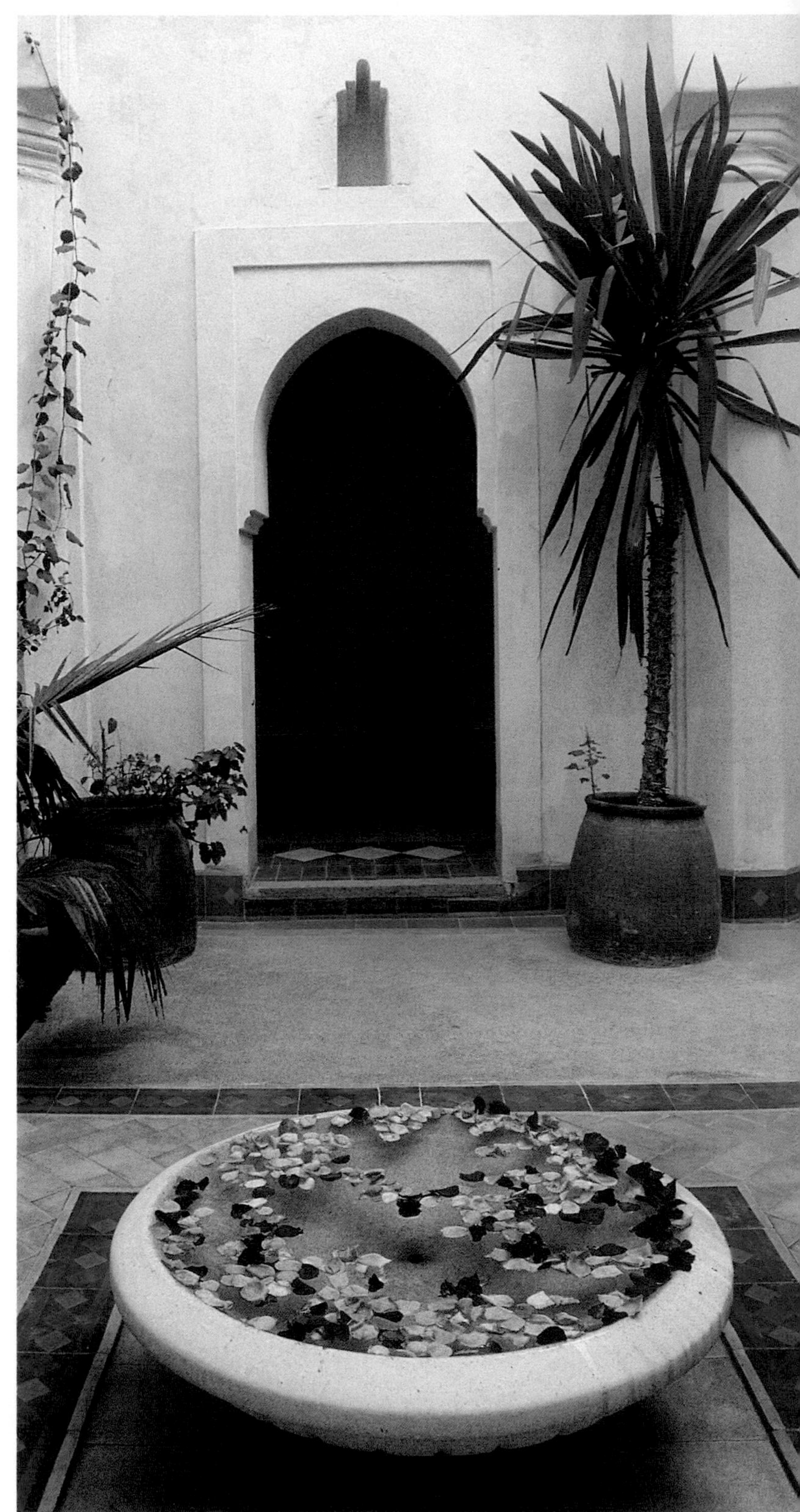

STATUARY AND URNS

The Mediterranean garden incorporates many architectural elements like paving and statuary, whereas in cooler climates more emphasis tends to be placed on the actual planting. The formal gardens of the Italian Renaissance can still inspire us today, renowned as they were for their innovative use of balustrades and terraces, statuary, fountains and cascades.

Traditionally, statuary and urns were used as a focus to draw the eye, and the placing of such pieces is as important as the object itself. A marble (or even reconstituted stone) sculpture is much more dramatic when outlined by the black-green of Italian cypresses, or when reflected in the still waters of a pool. Similarly, a large-scale stone or terracotta urn becomes an eye-catching focus if filled with brightly coloured flowers and set in the centre of a paved patio.

Stonework may also be used to introduce an element of surprise. Setting an animal mask or gargoyle into a plain expanse of wall brings it to life, and a stone figure or plant-filled pot situated just around a turn in a path will offer unexpected pleasure. Even the simplest garden schemes can benefit from such theatrical touches.

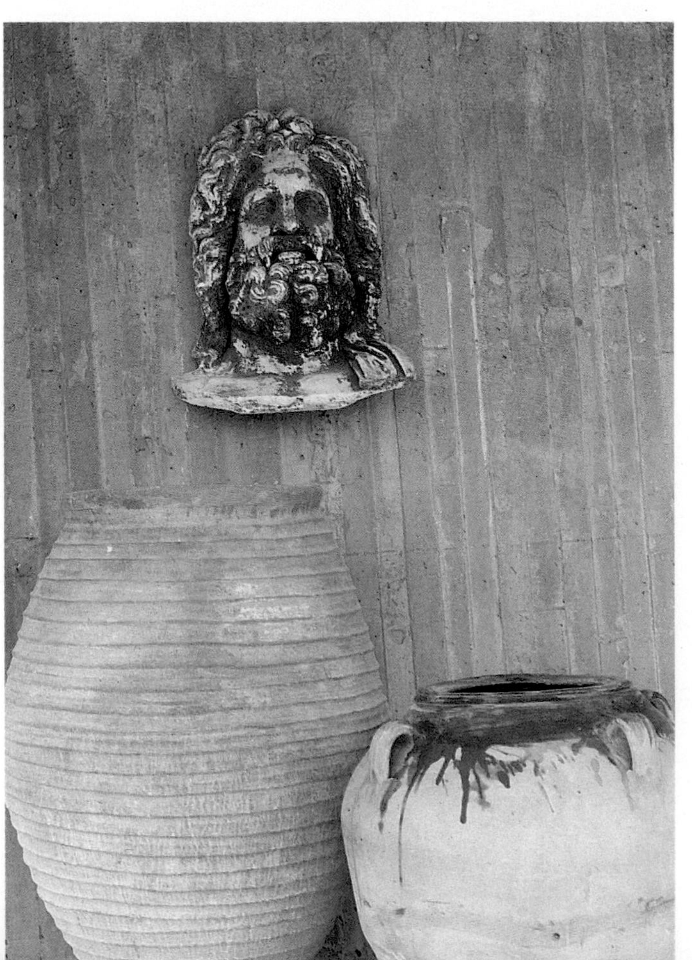

FLOORS AND PATHS

The Mediterranean house is so oriented towards life outside that there is a natural progression between the interior and the exterior decoration. Indeed, there is often no distinction between the two, and the sense of continuity is enhanced if the same materials are used throughout for the floors.

Hardwearing, natural materials predominate. They must be able to withstand both the occasional onslaught of wind and rain and the intense heat of summer. Thus, stone, brick, slate and even pebbles set into concrete are equally adaptable both inside and out. Wood is typically associated with balconies and verandahs or decks, whereas ceramic mosaics can add a splash of colour and pattern but, like terracotta tiles and wooden planks, are only suitable for covered or well-sheltered outdoor areas. Pebbles laid en masse like cobblestones, or in thick bands of contrasting colours, can be used to create patterns or accentuate particular garden features. Inset more sparingly, they allow the concrete base – left natural or coloured – to play a more dominant role.

Variations of texture and tone are used to define different spaces. Hence, a stone floor in an outdoor sitting or dining area might give way to a path of brick or gravel leading to the garden. Similarly, a brick floor might be laid in standard rectangular form on a patio but may break into herringbone patterns around a pool or flowerbed. Stone and brick weather well and mellow attractively with age. Any hard edges can be softened by planting in the crevices between them, providing the floor has been laid on sand rather than concrete.

Maintenance is an important practical consideration when choosing a floor covering. Stone and brick require only an occasional sweeping and perhaps a hose-down. Concrete

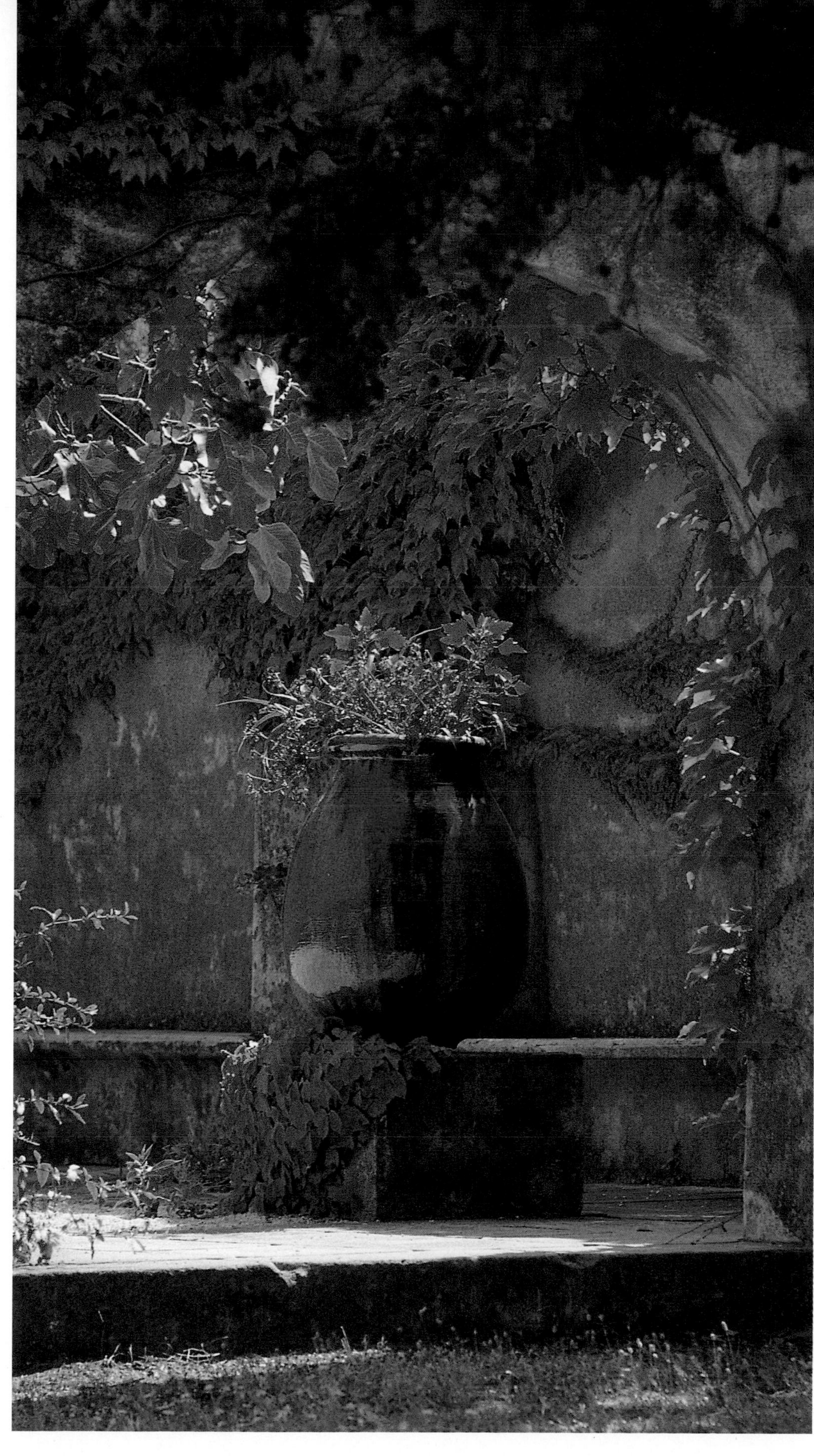

Left *A large ceramic pot creates an attractive focal point, its glossy glazed surface a striking contrast to the rough-textured wall behind. Planted with brightly coloured flowers it adds instant colour to an otherwise leafy setting.*

Facing *Two large terracotta urns and a terracotta bust form a balanced trio of ornaments. Mellowed with age, they make a pleasing composition, needing no embellishment of flowers or foliage.*

Left Regimented rows of pink geraniums and white petunias in simple, white-painted flowerpots look stunningly fresh and colourful on a three-tier jardinière, or plant stand.

Below right Make do and mend: a bright display spills out of a row of battered old tins and metal drums, eminently recyclable as serviceable containers for plants.

will prevent the growth of weeds but will also preclude any planting in the area. A wooden floor may become slippery unless regularly scrubbed, while tiles must be set into a firm concrete base to survive wear and tear. If they are not set correctly cracks and chips will rapidly appear.

CONTAINERS

No Mediterranean terrace or patio is complete without some form of container gardening, and the choice and adaptation of these containers show extraordinary style and ingenuity, ranging from the elegantly grand to the humbly simple. Old terracotta jars and urns are imposing both in terms of their size and grandeur. Originally used for olive oil or water, or even in the production of wine, they exemplify indigenous craftsmanship. They are beautifully shaped, with surfaces that are either ridged or smooth, sometimes semi-glazed or unglazed, and they may also still have their original handles. Although they are intrinsically rustic, they can provide an imposing focal point in any setting.

Terracotta flowerpots also come in a variety of shapes and sizes. Some are deliberately kept plain, while others benefit from simple surface decoration. All weather attractively to a soft, mellow tone. Alternatively, they can be painted to co-ordinate or contrast with the surroundings. Exceptionally versatile, they can be used individually or en masse to create dramatically diverse effects.

Old troughs and rainwater tanks in either stone or wood make decorative containers for larger plantings. On a smaller scale, all sorts of unlikely objects can be used as containers: old olive-oil cans, with their lids or tops removed; terracotta chimneypots; metal or enamel buckets; ceramic dishes and jugs. Mediterranean ingenuity knows no bounds – as witnessed by the plethora of pots appearing on every doorstep and window sill whenever there is a shower of rain.

Container gardening is easily adaptable to non-Mediterranean countries and can be an effective way to add a Mediterranean feel to a garden. Little space is required and potted plants allow more scope for seasonal variation in the garden. The same criteria applies when choosing pots for either climate. Pots should be sympathetic in style to their surroundings; they need to have provision for drainage, with a layer of stones or broken crockery in the base; and they must have sufficient depth to give the roots good cover, especially in hot weather. Drying out is a problem and, as the roots tend to gather around the outside of the soil for better aeration, they are particularly vulnerable to overheating and drought. The choice of material can help: clay allows evaporation, helping to keep temperatures down, whereas black plastic simply absorbs and retains the heat. Place the pots in the shade if possible or mass them together so that the larger ones shade the smaller ones.

Tools & Materials

- Terracotta pots – diameter approx. 15 cm (6 in)
- Power drill and masonry bit
- 10 cm (4 in) large-headed masonry nails, wall plugs and hammer
- Scraps of wood and a handsaw
- 5 cm (2 in) masonry nails
- Gloss paint and paintbrush
- Primer (general-purpose or alkali-resistant)
- Broken crockery and potting soil (compost)

Choose an appropriate number of terracotta pots. These should be about 15 cm (6 in) in diameter – large enough for the growing plant, but not too heavy to hang on the wall when filled with soil. Lightweight potting soil (compost) is available for hanging baskets. If you intend to leave the terracotta pots outdoors all year, check that they are frostproof before purchasing them.

To create an authentic look, the pots should be hung on a white-painted, preferably plastered, wall and filled with colourful flowers. We used pelargoniums, which are easy to grow in pots and flourish in warm conditions. Impatiens and some types of begonia may also be used.

Method

● Using a power drill with a masonry bit, make a hole 1 cm (½ in) below the

Painted Terracotta Wall Pots

rim of the pot 1. The hole should be just larger than the head of the nail from which the pot is to be hung.

- Drill a pilot hole for the nail and insert a wall plug. Hammer the nail into the hole, allowing it to extend just enough for the pot to be hung easily but securely.
- Cut a block of wood no wider than the base of the pot. Drill and plug a pilot hole in the wall in line with the base of the pot and position the wood over the hole. Hammer it firmly in place. (You may find it easier to make a pilot hole in the wood first, using a bradawl.) The block acts as a wedge, ensuring that the pot hangs straight and does not tilt towards the wall.
- Apply a coat of primer to the outside of the pot, and allow to dry before painting the pot 2. Primary colours will work best against a white wall.
- Repeat the process for as many wall pots as you require. Allow the pots to dry overnight before planting.

Planting

- Cover the drainage hole at the bottom of the pot with broken crockery, which will keep the soil from blocking the hole and becoming waterlogged.
- Fill the base of the pot with potting soil, put the plant inside and cover the roots with soil, pressing down gently but firmly. Fill the pot with soil, leaving a space of about 2.5 cm (1 in) at the top.
- Water the plants well after potting and continue to water frequently throughout the flowering period, but especially while the plants are taking root 3.

Left *Red pelargoniums combine with a profusion of greenery and a vivid blue distemper for a tropical effect.*

OUTDOOR ENTERTAINING

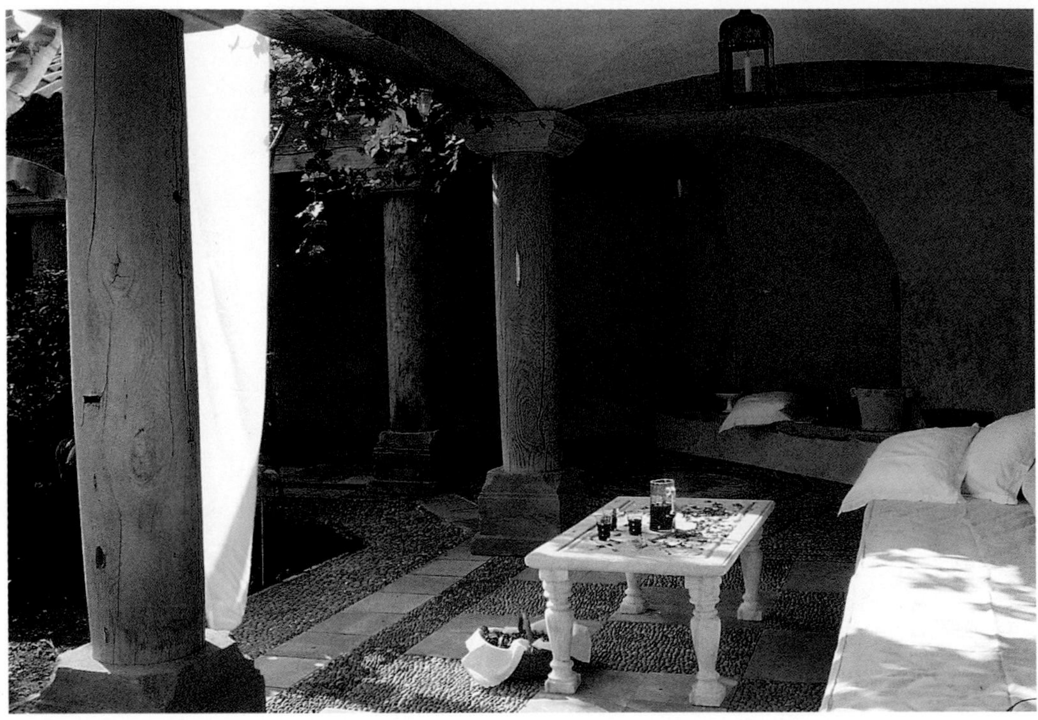

Above Cushioned banquettes make the most of a covered cloister, while allowing a view of the garden beyond. A sturdy wooden table provides space for drinks and food.

Facing Inset ceramic tiles, complete with decorative border, are a durable and easy-to-clean surface that is ideal for an outdoor table; weatherproof in all conditions except the heaviest frost.

An outdoor room is a natural setting for entertaining. Shaded by plants and lulled by the sound of water or the soothing murmur of the sea, mealtimes become a magical experience. Whether the occasion is a simple family lunch or a formal dinner, this is Mediterranean life at its best.

DINING FURNITURE

When buying outdoor furniture, it is important to choose a style that is in keeping with the size and character of the outdoor 'room'. Any furniture should also be able to withstand the elements. A sturdy refectory table would be appropriate for a narrow terrace or pergola and solid enough to stand up to the onslaught of sun and wind. It will also weather gently with the passing seasons. Pair it with heavy farmhouse chairs, with wicker or wooden seats.

A round wrought-iron table on decoratively curved legs, which could be moved easily to make the most of sun and shade, might better suit a small, enclosed courtyard.

Matching metal chairs with removable cushions would make a weatherproof combination, although metal can become uncomfortably hot to touch in the strong sun.

Trestle tables and folding chairs are the most flexible option, allowing meals to be served wherever they are required. On a hot day the table might be set in deep shade in a covered courtyard; in the evening it could be moved to take advantage of the refreshing sound of a fountain or the scent of particular plants. Out of season, when other outdoor furniture might have been stored away, it can be set up on a sunny day in a sheltered corner of the garden.

Outdoor areas with solid walls on one or more sides have the potential for a built-in seat or banquette, which will free up valuable space and allow the dining table to be moved further into the shade. A banquette usually seats more people than conventional dining chairs so is especially useful when entertaining large groups of people. Depending on the materials used for the house, a banquette might be made of moulded concrete, stone blocks or wood. Ideally, it should have seat pads and scatter cushions for comfort.

A solid wall may also provide the opportunity of installing an outdoor fireplace, particularly if one of the existing chimneys can be used. The warmth and light given out by an open fire adds an extra dimension to outdoor living and can extend the use of an outside sitting or dining area by several weeks in spring and autumn when the evenings can be distinctly chilly.

Smaller, occasional tables provide useful surface space for setting down trays laden with food or drinks. Equally, a narrow console table or sideboard, placed against one wall, could serve the same purpose. Tiling the top – either conventionally or as a mosaic – helps to create a hygienic and easy-to-clean surface, and adds a welcome splash of colour as well.

Decorating the table

Thanks to imaginative planting and the favourable climate, most Mediterranean outdoor rooms are settings of such natural beauty that the decoration of the table becomes secondary. Attention will inevitably be drawn away from the table by a wisteria in full bloom, a pot brimming over with colour, a statue or a fountain. The most successful table arrangements are those that complement the surroundings rather than compete with them. Hand-painted ceramics, chunky French wine glasses and brightly printed cotton table linen, for example, all draw on the craftsmanship of the region.

Simple use of colour can be very effective: blue-and-white china might be offset by blue glass and a combination of blue and white linen. Alternatively, the reds and greens of the surrounding planting could be reproduced in green leaf plates, red checked napkins and dark red wine glasses. Sunny yellows, contrasted with bright shades of aquamarine, lime or orange, will echo the sun-saturated palette of the garden beyond. A crisp white damask tablecloth instantly adds a sense of formality, matched perhaps with white napkins and fine china, while a brightly checked, striped or patterned fabric suggests a more relaxed occasion.

Left *This delightful table arrangement combines fresh fruit in a natural woven bowl, with a simple but attractive jug and chunky glasses. Relaxed informality is the result.*

Right *Elegantly rustic garden furniture forms the basis of this attractive table arrangement. Grapes fresh from the vine add a touch of sophistication, while the vine motif is picked up in the design of the dishes and garden chair.*

Flowers and foliage are natural subjects for table decoration. A simple bunch of country flowers in a pottery jug looks uncontrived, while particularly beautiful blooms, such as parrot tulips or roses, can be shown to best effect by putting only two or three stems in a glass vase. Foliage can be used with flowers, or can be just as effective used alone.

Fruit and vegetables in season are another rich resource. For a typically Mediterranean look, use those with bright skins or flesh. Lemons or limes piled high in a colourful ceramic bowl, a glass dish of strawberries or cherries, and a plate of purple figs all make stunning and edible table arrangements. Vegetables such as artichokes, feathery fennel root or tiny cherry tomatoes are colourful and decorative, while simply lining a plate, bowl or basket with vine or fig leaves adds an element of natural greenery.

Living plants may also be incorporated into the table decoration. A row of bright geraniums in painted terracotta pots would enliven a long table. Flowering daisies or fuchsias, used singly or in groups, are also characteristic of the region. Vary the containers to suit the occasion and be prepared to adapt table arrangements as the different species come into bloom.

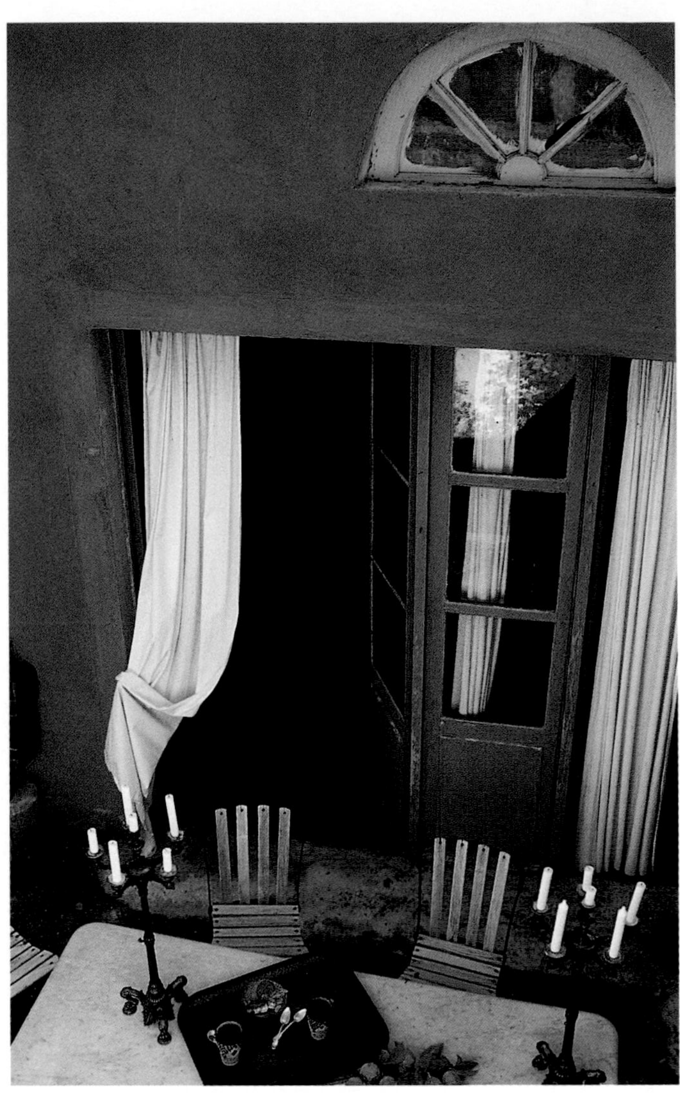

Above *Striking contrasts: a marble-topped table is set with slatted wooden chairs, while the simple centrepiece of fruit and leaves is flanked by a pair of antique candelabra.*

Facing *A wisteria in full bloom provides the crowning glory for a fresh, summery table setting. A pair of storm lanterns is the only additional decorative touch, apart from a sprinkling of purple petals.*

Lighting

Long, warm summer evenings mean that people eat out of doors long after sunset in the Mediterranean and some sort of artificial lighting is therefore essential. Candlelight is the most obvious solution and, on a still night, nothing looks prettier than its flickering glow. If the patio or terrace has a solid or beamed roof, candles can be suspended above the table in lanterns or chandeliers. An array of different candleholders could be placed on the table itself, from night lights in saucers through to tall, slender candlesticks in wood, ceramic or metal. Candelabra look elegant, and a row of storm lanterns is both effective and decorative. Make sure that candle flames are kept away from any plants, otherwise they may be damaged. There are specially made holders for combining candles and flowers. Alternatively, anchor a candle in oasis (florist's foam) and fill in around the base with flowers or foliage: terracotta flowerpots make good containers. Citronella candles smell delicious and are useful insect deterrents.

In recent years outdoor lighting has become something of an art form, with more and more gardens benefiting from the subtle and theatrical effects of a well-designed lighting scheme. A combination of concealed uplighters and wall-hung lanterns could be used to create a soft, ambient glow around an outdoor dining room. In addition, carefully focused lights might draw attention to a special feature, such as a fine statue, or pot, or a mature cypress. Such techniques are used widely in the Mediterranean region but can work wonderfully in any setting, even in cooler climates where eating outside is a rare luxury. Illuminating the garden brings it into focus from the dining area, whether it is on a terrace, in a conservatory, or inside the house. Wiring and fittings for outdoor lighting need to be safety-approved, and it is advisable to consider professional installation.

SOURCES

UNITED KINGDOM

GENERAL

After Noah
121 Upper St
London
N1 1QP
Tel: 0171 379 6254

The Conran Shop
Michelin House
81 Fulham Road
London
SW3 6RD
Tel: 0171 589 7401

Global Village
4th Floor
Harvey Nichols
109-125 Knightsbridge
London SW1
Tel: 0171 235 5000

Habitat
196 Tottenham Court Rd
London
W1P 9LD
Tel: 0171 255 2545

Ikea
2 Drury Lane
Brent Park
North Circular Rd
London
NW10 0TH
Tel: 0181 451 5566

John Lewis
Oxford Street
London
W1A 1EX
Tel: 0171 629 7711
(And branches throughout the UK.)

The Kasbah
8 Southampton St
Covent Garden
London WC2
Tel: 0171 379 5230

Natural Fact
192 King's Road
London
SW3 5XP
Tel: 0171 352 2227

FLOORING AND TILES

Crucial Trading
77 Westbourne Park Road
London
W2 4BX
Tel: 0171 221 9000
(Natural matting.)

Elon
66 Fulham Road
London
SW3 6HH
Tel: 0171 584 8966
(Terracotta, slate, glazed floor and wall tiles.)

Etrusca
60 Dickson House
Ridgeway Road
Harley
Stoke-on-Trent
Staffordshire
ST1 3PA
Tel: 01782 208549
(handpainted ceramic tiles, panels, mirrors.)

European Heritage Ltd.
56 Dawes Road
London
SW6 7EJ
Tel: 0171 381 6063
(Natural stone, terracotta, ceramic, marble and handpainted tiles.)

Fired Earth
Twyford Mill
Oxford Road
Adderbury
Oxon
OX17 3HP
Tel: 01295 812088
(Tiles.)

The Hardwood Flooring Co., Ltd.
146/152 West End Lane
West Hampstead
London NW6
Tel: 0171 328 8481
(New and reclaimed parquet-block and strip flooring.)

Natural Carpets
Oak House
Baughurst
Basingstoke
Hants
RG26 5LP
Tel: 01345 585323
(Seagrass, coir, sisal and wool flatweave flooring.)

Paris Ceramics
583 King's Road
London SW6
Tel: 0171 371 7778
and
4 Montpellier Walk
Harrogate
N. Yorkshire
Tel: 01423 523877
(Stone, terracotta, ceramic and marble tiles.)

Rugstore
637 Fulham Road
London
SW6 5UQ
Tel: 0171 610 9800
(New and antique kilims, carpets, rugs, runners, kilim cushions, kilim upholstered furniture.)

Stonell Ltd.
Unit 1, Bockingfold
Ladham Road
Goudhurst
Kent
TN17 1LY
Tel: 01580 211167
(Limestone, slate, marble, sandstone, granite.)

Three Shires Natural Flooring
3 Ptarmigan Place
Attleborough
Nuneaton
Warwickshire
CB11 6RX
Tel: 01203 370365
(Sisal, seagrass, coir, wool.)

PAINTS

Brats
281 Kings Road
London
SW3 5EW
Tel: 0171 351 7674
(Stock a range of paints based on the Mediterranean palette.)

Nutshell Natural Paints
Hamlyn House
Buckfastleigh
Devon TQ11 0NR
Tel: 01364 642892
(Natural distemper and limewash.)

Omnihome
77 Golbourne Road
London
W10 5NP
Tel: 0181 964 2100
(Including a Mediterranean-inspired paint range.)

Paint Library
5 Elyston Street
Chelsea Green
London
SW3 3NT
Tel: 0171 823 7755
(Mediterranean-inspired colours in various finishes.)

Paint Magic
116 Sheen Road
Richmond
Surrey
TW9 1UR
Tel: 0181 940 5503
(Including liming paste and washes.)

Furnishings and Display

Damask
3-4 Broxholme House
New Kings Road
Nr Harwood Road
London SW6
Tel: 0171 731 3553
(Pure cotton bedlinen.)

The London Shutter Company
Tel: 01344 28385
Fax: 01344 27575
(Made to measure shutters.)

Lunn Antiques
86 New Kings Road
London
SW6 4LU
Tel: 0171 736 4638
(Antique linen and cotton.)

The Monogrammed Linen Shop
168 Walton Street
London
SW3 2JL
Tel: 0171 589 4033
(100% cotton and linen bedlinen and fabrics.)

The Natural Fabric Co.,
Wessex Place
127 High Street
Hungerford
Berkshire
RG17 0DL
Tel: 01488 684002
(Calico, ticking, cotton and voile.)

Garden Statuary and Urns

The Bulbeck Foundry
Reach Road
Burwell
Cambridgeshire
CB5 0AH
(A range of lead fountains, urns, garden fittings and statuary.)

Chelsea Gardener
125 Sydney Street
London
SW3 6NR
Tel: 0171 352 5656
(Urns, statuary, stoneware and furniture.)

Garden Art
25 Queen Street
The Quayside
Newcastle-upon-Tyne
NE1 3UG
Tel: 0191 232 6360
(Terracotta urns, iron benches, classical statues, marble cobbles.)

Pots and Pithoi
The Barns
East Street (B2110)
Turners Hill
West Sussex
Tel: 01342 714793
(Pots handmade in Crete.)

Seago
22 Pimlico Road
London
SW1W 8LJ
Tel: 0171 730 7502
(Antique garden sculpture.)

Victoria's Collection Ltd.
Maltby House
London Road
Louth
Lincolnshire
LN11 9QP
Tel: 01507 609212
(Specialists in antique terracotta. *Viewings by appointment only.*)

Australia

Dulux Australia
McNaughton Road
Clayton
Victoria 2123

Home Hardware
414 Lower Dandenong Road
Braeside
Victoria 3195

McEwans
387-403 Bourke Street
Melbourne
Victoria 3000

Canada

The Home Depot, Canada
Store Support Centre
426 Ellesmere Road
Scarborough
Ontario
M1R 4E7

Ikea
15 Provost Dr.
North York
Ontario
M2K 2X9

Up Country
247 Kind St. E
Toronto
Ontario
M5A 1J9

New Zealand

Cottage Ironwork
82 The Mall
Onehunga
Auckland

Garden Bronze Co.,
26 Ashfield Street
Glenfield
Auckland

Hibiscus Coast Tile Warehouse
Unit D
5 Agency Lane
Silverdale

Levene & Co., Ltd.
68 Harris Road
East Tamaki
Auckland

Ornamentally Yours
12 Princes Street
Onehunga
Auckland

Static Beauty NZ
Unit 8/2, Margan Avenue
New Lynn
Auckland

South Africa

Flora Farm Garden City
General Retail Nursery
11 North Rand Road
Bartletts
Boksburg 1459

Home Warehouse
Johannesburg (Edenvale)
Dick Kemp Street
Meadowdale
Ext. 6

Parker Floors
PO Box 1071
Jukskei Park

Sun Ray Canopies
Tel: (011) 836 9415/8

Tate Access Floor Systems Pty Ltd
All Black Road
Boksburg North 1461
Gauteng

Tile City
31-33 Sivewright Avenue
New Doornfontein
Johannesburg

Universal Paints
Johannesburg - Randburg
24 Hendrick Verwoerd Drive
Cnr Dalmeny Road, Linden

INDEX

Page numbers in *italic* refer to illustrations; those in **bold** refer to the practical projects.

ACKNOWLEDGMENTS

AUTHOR'S ACKNOWLEDGMENTS

I would like to thank the team at Conran Octopus, in particular Helen Wire, for their hard work on this project. I also owe a big thank you to Peter, William, Georgiana and Rachel for all their tolerance and support.

PUBLISHER'S ACKNOWLEDGMENTS

We would like to thank the following photographers and organizations for their permission to reproduce the photographs in this book.

1 Eric Morin ; 2 -3 Lisl Dennis/The Image Bank; 4 -5 Roland Beaufre (J. Pascal)/Marie Claire Maison; 6 -7 Marc Romanelli/The Image Bank; 8 Simon McBride; 9 Lisl Dennis/The Image Bank; 10 Mads Mogensen; 11 Earl Carter; 12 Carlos Navajas/The Image Bank; 13 Christian Sarramon; 14 Carlos Navajas/The Image Bank; 15 P. Wysocki/ Explorer; 16 Jean-Pierre Godeaut; 17 Marc Romanelli/The Image Bank; 18 Michel Dayez; 19 Earl Carter; 20 -21 Carlos Navajas/The Image Bank; 21 Lisl Dennis/The Image Bank; 22 Guy Bouchet/Inside; 23-24 Deidi von Schaewen (Joel Martial); 25 Gilles de Chabaneix (C. Ardouin)/Marie Claire Maison; 26 -27 Rene Stoeltie; 28 Fritz von der Schulenburg/The Interior Archive; 29 Dexter Hodges/La Casa de Marie Claire; 30 Jean-Pierre Godeaut; 31 Paul Ryan (D & V Tsingaris)/International Interiors; 32 -33 Marie-Pierre Morel (D. Rozensztroch)/Marie Claire Maison; 33 Jean-Pierre Godeaut; 34 Deidi von Schaewen (Architect: Chantel Schaler); 35 Tim Beddow/The Interior Archive; 37 Alexandre Bailhache (C. Ardouin)/Marie Claire Maison; 38 Deidi von Schaewen (Xavier Guerrand Hermes); 39 Marie-Pierre Morel (D. Rozensztroch)/Marie Claire Maison; 40 Lisl Dennis/The Image Bank; 41 Pierre Hussenot/Agence Top; 42 -43 Roland Beaufre/Agence Top; 43 Marie-Pierre (D. Rozensztroch)/Marie Claire Maison; 45 Marianne Majerus (Colombe d'Or, St Paul de vence); 46 Deidi von Schaewen (Architect: Quentin Wilbaux); 47 Yves Duronsoy/Inside; 48 Fritz von der Schulenburg/The Interior Archive; 49 Fritz von der Schulenburg/The Interior Archive; 50 Pascal Chevalier/Agence Top; 51 Andreas von Einsiedel/Elizabeth Whiting and Associates; 53-54 Antonio Maniscalco; 55 Paul Ryan(D & V Tsingaris) /International Interiors; 56 Jean-Pierre Godeaut; 57 Deidi von Schaewen (Architect: Quentin Wilbaux); 58 -59 Ianthe Ruthven; 60 Fritz von der Schulenburg/The Interior Archive; 60 -61 Deidi von Schaewen (Xavier Guerrand Hermes); 62 Roland Beaufre (Architect Charles Boccara)/Agence Top; 63 Pierre Hussenot/ Agence Top; 64 Ianthe Ruthven ; 65 Deidi von Schaewen; 67 J. P. Lagarde/Inside; 68 Simon McBride; 69 Janos Grapow; 70 Marie Pierre Morel (C.Puech)/Marie Claire Maison; 70 -71 Antonio Maniscalco; 72 Christophe Dugied (A.M. Comte)/Marie Claire Maison; 73 Marie Pierre Morel (C. Puech)/Marie Claire Maison; 76 John Miller; 77 above Roland Beaufre (Architect Stuart Church)/Agence Top; 77 Below Roland Beaufre (J.P. Billaud)/Marie Claire Maison; 78 Dominique Silberstein/ Agence Top; 79 John Miller; 81 Deidi von Schaewen; 82-83 Antonio Maniscalco; 84 Jerome Darblay (C von Rosen)/Inside; 85 Solvi Dos Santos; 86 Eric Morin ; 87 Jean-Pierre Godeaut (Yuri Kuper)/ Inside; 90 G. Bouchet/Inside; 91 Antonio Maniscalco; 94 -95 Gilles de Chabaneix (C.Ardouin)/ Marie Claire Maison; 95 Jean-Pierre Godeaut; 97 Andreas von Einsiedel/Elizabeth Whiting & Associates; 98 Alexandre Bailhache (C.Ardouin)/Marie Claire Maison; 99 Fritz von der Schulenburg (Miani D'Angors)/ The Interior Archive; 100 -101 Pascal Chevallier/Agence Top; 102 -103 Simon McBride; 104 Gilles de Chabaneix (C.Ardouin)/Marie Claire Maison; 105 left Fritz von der Schulenburg/The Interior Archive; 105 right Deidi von Schaewen (Mr & Mrs Dusots la Chartre, designer: Charles Chauliagues); 106 Jean-Pierre Godeaut; 107 Marie Pierre Morel (D. Rozensztroch)/ Marie Claire Maison; 110 -111 Christian Sarramon; 112 Deidi von Schaewen (Mr & Mrs Dusots la Chartre, designer: Charles Chauliagues); 113 Marie Pierre Morel (D. Rozensztroch)/Marie Claire Maison; 114 -115 Fritz von der Schulenburg/The Interior Archive; 116 -117 Fritz von der Schulenburg/The Interior Archive; 117 right Christian Sarramon; 118 Weinberg/Clark/ The Image Bank; 119 Antonio Maniscalco; 120-121 Eric Morin; 122 Jerome Darblay/Inside; 123 left Rene Stoeltie; 123 right John Miller; 124 Antoine Rozes; 125 Jean-Pierre Godeaut (Jacqueline Foissac); 126 J C Mayer - G Le Scanff (J. Majorelk, Marrakech); 127 Deidi von Schaewen (Architect: Quentin Wilbaux); 128 Antoine Rozes; 129 Pierre Hussenot/Agence Top; 130 Fritz von der Schulenburg/The Interior Archive; 131 Nevada Wier/The Image Bank; 132 Polly Farquharson/ The World of Interiors; 133 Verne Fotografie; 134 Christian Sarramon; 134 -135 Gilles de Chabaneix (C. Ardouin)/Marie Claire Maison; 136 -137 Christian Sarramon (H. Thibault); 137 Pierre Hussenot(Domaine de Tempiers)/ Agence Top; 138 Christian Sarramon (H.Thibault); 139 Tim Clinch/The Interior Archive.

The photographs on the following pages were taken specially for Conran Octopus by Hannah Lewis, projects produced by Emily Jewsbury: pp. 36, 44, 52, 68, 74, 87, 92, 96, 108.